DISCARD

SystemKids

Adolescent Mothers and the Politics of Regulation

LAUREN J. SILVER

The University of North Carolina Press CHAPEL HILL

This book was published with the assistance of the Authors Fund of the
University of North Carolina Press.

Set in Utopia and Aller types by codeMantra
Manufactured in the United States of America

The paper in this book meets the guidelines for permanence
and durability of the Committee on Production Guidelines for Book
Longevity of the Council on Library Resources. The University of
North Carolina Press has been a member of the Green Press Initiative
since 2003.

Jacket illustration: Photograph of street mural by
Geoff Andruik, www.geoffandruik.com.

Library of Congress Cataloging-in-Publication Data
Silver, Lauren J.
System kids : adolescent mothers and the politics of regulation / Lauren J. Silver.
    pages cm
Includes bibliographical references and index.
ISBN 978-1-4696-2259-0 (pbk : alk. paper) — ISBN 978-1-4696-2260-6 (ebook)
1. Teenage mothers—United States. 2. Child welfare—United States. 3. Aid to
families with dependent children programs—United States. 4. Maternal and
infant welfare—United States. I. Title.
HQ759.4.S537 2015
362.7′874300973—dc23
2014031683

Portions of this work have appeared previously, in somewhat different
form, as "Minding the Gap: Adolescent Mothers Navigate Child
Welfare," *Social Science Review* 82, no. 4 (2008): 615–38, and "Spaces
of Encounter: Public Bureaucracy and the Making of Child Identities,"
Ethos 38, no. 3 (2010): 275–96.

This book was digitally printed

Dedicated to those
who have generously shared
their stories

Contents

Acknowledgments

Your silence will not protect you.—Audre Lorde

Many have supported me in the writing of this book. I have often feared whether I would "get it right," because I wanted this book to do justice to the youth and providers who shared their experiences with me. Remaining silent, however, was never an option. I am first and foremost thankful to the young moms and service providers who welcomed me into their lives and their homes, shared their stories, and let me accompany them to court, schools, medical clinics, and numerous other sites across their large northeastern city. I learned more from them than they will ever know. Even though I cannot mention any of the participants by their actual names (just as I cannot name the city where they live), their voices are present and unique; they make up the heart and soul of this book. This book stems from their collective visions of hope and persistence against constraints. I am humbled by the openness and generosity of these young women and their families. It was truly an honor to spend time with them and to get to know them. After many years, I continue to be inspired by their courage, integrity, and willingness to share their stories.

Friends often compared the process of writing this book to giving birth, and the gestation has indeed been long. The birth of this book was only possible through the help and support of many people, across several phases of development. I want to thank my advisors who guided me during the earliest research and writing phase: Kathleen Hall, Katherine Schultz, Margaret Beale Spencer, and Vivian Gadsden. I will never forget the hours, days, and months spent with my writing partner, Cheryl Jones-Walker. The glances of encouragement as she sat across the table from me helped me continue writing that next page. For their encouragement and advice more recently, I want to thank my wonderful Rutgers University colleagues Daniel

Hart, Susan Miller, Robin Stevens, Lynne Vallone, and especially Daniel Cook, a wonderful mentor, who read and provided feedback on an entire draft of the book. Dan Cook, thank you for the frozen yogurt at that key moment in the process. I owe much appreciation to my brilliant writing group and dear friends whose keen insights motivated me and made this book possible: Elizabeth Davis, Jessica Goldberg, Belinda Haikes, Pamela Mazzeo, and Melissa Yates.

I am incredibly fortunate to have a generous editor, Joseph Parsons, who understands the book on a deep level and respects me as an author. Joe's confidence in the project inspired me to take important risks with the manuscript. I am also grateful for his selection of committed readers and for the scholars whose detailed insights helped me to clarify the arguments and the contributions of the book. I am thankful for the efforts of many individuals at UNC Press who made the publication and distribution of this book possible. I appreciate the close copyediting provided by Romaine Perin before my final submission of the manuscript to UNC Press and her heartfelt comments about the book's relevance. Romaine reminded me that stories could be meaningful to audiences in powerful ways that we as authors could never foresee.

I want to thank my family and friends whose encouragement provided the loving foundation for me to do this work. They reminded me of three important themes throughout the process of bringing this book to fruition: trust, perseverance, and patience. In particular, I want to thank my mother, Marilyn Silver; my stepfather, Donald Coates; my brother, Justin Silver; my sister-in-law, Jaime Silver; and my dear friends Hanne Harbison, Anna Koopman, Helen Lee, Joanna Lee, Amy Mahlke, Craig Mahlke, Angela McIver, and Gail Wolfe. Finally, I especially want to thank my wife, Raïssa Schickel, whose love and belief in the project provided such a force of support and constancy. Thank you, Raï, for your patience, the delicious meals, and keeping our household afloat while I wrote this book.

SystemKids

They Want to See You Fail

Dilemmas in Child Welfare

Soon after sundown, in the dimly lit front room of her inner-city apartment, eighteen-year-old Maleka told me about registering for nursing school and the challenges she faced with childcare. All the while, Maleka repeatedly swatted at her wall with a towel, keeping the scurrying roaches from making their way down to her two boys, playing on a secondhand couch. The swatting seemed so habitual that I wondered whether this was something she repeated every evening. It did not distract her from our conversation, nor did it bother her two boys, who continued to play.

This simple, disturbing act represents the many extraordinary, but seemingly minor, efforts of young mothers to protect their children. Maleka lived alone with her sons in an apartment leased by a Supervised Independent Living (SIL) program. The local child welfare agency, Children and Youth Services (CYS), funded this program through a government contract and expected SIL to facilitate residential, educational, and social services.[1] In spite of the dangerous environments and bureaucratic obstacles they encountered on entering the child welfare system, young mothers in SIL persevered. I came to know the SIL program and its young families first as a program manager with concrete responsibilities and then later as a researcher who continued to advocate for clients.

Once the child welfare system assumes legal custody of abused or neglected youth, the youth are *in care* and the government provides for their well-being. How do we understand the "care" provided, given the circumstances that Maleka and her children and many other young families face? How would an adolescent's living alone with her children in dangerous and pest-infested conditions satisfy any parent's wishes for his or her child's well-being, let alone meet the legal mandates of the state? How does the state normalize program conditions for these particular children and youth, who simultaneously occupy several categories of disadvantage?

The inspiration for this book came from young mothers' voices.[2] Youth in SIL shared with me stories of survival despite abuse, homelessness, rape, failed suicide attempts, imprisonment, dropping out of school, and abandonment. This book resists media and scholarly representations that decontextualize and stereotype marginalized young people as flat, culturally deficient characters who act in violent and deceitful ways that white, middle-class citizens cannot understand. These distorted representations follow a long tradition in the United States of making the racial Other into a spectacle for general consumption and positioning those with access to dominant culture as normative (Alonso et al. 2009; Farley 2002; Rios 2011).

Mothers expressed dynamic visions for their futures. The SIL program's mission rhetorically reflected the mothers' objectives: to "provide temporary housing and comprehensive services to low-income teen girls and their families to help them achieve economic independence and family well-being." In spite of these laudable goals, youth aspirations were largely unfulfilled, in part because of barriers within the child welfare system and its programs. Young families faced challenges within the system, and these exacerbated the obstacles of living in impoverished and racially segregated urban communities. This book reveals why and how the child welfare system compromises its own mission of promoting the well-being of young families.

Scholars offer powerful, historically documented narratives about changes in the nature of U.S. cities through demographic, economic, political, and social shifts that cause divestment, in particular in inner-city neighborhoods (Dreier, Mollenkopf, and Swanstrom 2004; Kantor and Brenzel 1992; Sugrue 1999). Families and children shoulder massive burdens as mass incarceration removes parents from the home and disconnects them from mainstream institutions (Alexander 2012; Beckett and Western 2001; Davis 2003; Haney 2004; Wacquant 2002). No clear border separates child welfare interventions and the urban environments in which these programs function; rather, this book shows how inequalities within bureaucratic systems mirror and perpetuate racial, gendered, and class-based divisions in the city and society. We need to understand how families experience child welfare interventions in the context of continuing urban poverty, violence, and racial segregation. Only then can we foresee what are often labeled as the "unforeseen" implications of public policies concerning children and youth.

Once the state takes custody of a young mother, her care and that of her children become fragmented, distributed among different urban bureaucracies, including health, mental health, educational, and residential systems. In the process, these systems turn individuals into managed "cases," causing youth to shift between identities—as mothers, delinquents, dependents, clients, patients, students, and workers. Scholars generally investigate these populations as separate entities, when in actuality youth tend to occupy simultaneous and shifting statuses.[3] As youth move across system settings, they deploy creative strategies that, when considered in isolation, cannot be recognized by policymakers, practitioners, and the public. Nor do we get a sense of the burdens experienced by youth who must negotiate multiple institutions and identities at once. Research on these populations tends to be quantitative in design (Smith 2011). I address substantive and methods gaps in the scholarship and use ethnography to learn *how* youth experience multiple system settings and *why* youth face challenges negotiating their identities.

Throughout the book, I refer to the young participants through changing characterizations, as *young mothers, adolescent moms, clients,* and *youth*. I do this deliberately to emphasize the fluidity of their multiple identities and to signify the distinct effects of different social labels. This book highlights the trajectories of youth across settings in order to emphasize the strategies of youth themselves. As they act as navigators of multiple systems, their narratives challenge popular conceptions of poor "disconnected youth," suggesting instead that institutions structure fragmentation. The ethnographic form reconstitutes and recaptures the coherence of youth narratives. It is not that their daily lives are unintelligible but, rather, that fragmented systems project disjointed representations.

To understand youth trajectories, it is essential to contextualize the roles and decisions of caseworkers. Throughout the book,

I use the terms *caseworker* and *case manager* interchangeably. Officials across institutions did not usually trust youth; therefore, caseworkers were charged with acting on their behalf while negotiating health care, childcare, and other services for youth. Youth and their caseworkers struggled to manage the gap between formal stipulations and the informal realities of underresourced, stigmatized, and dangerous program contexts. For instance, although the SIL program and CYS system expected youth to participate in an educational program, these organizations did not provide many clients with childcare resources. Further, moms were either afraid or unable to leave their children with friends or family members in unsafe SIL apartment buildings. As we will see, youth and their caseworkers worked together to manage an impression of a client's educational compliance when the institutions responsible for the youth's care did not coordinate supports for actual compliance. By delving into the daily work experiences of caseworkers, this book offers a needed account of how they too were trapped within the system. Clients and officials across levels shared feelings of entrapment. However, daily experiences of these restrictions varied, because access to power shaped the stakes in vastly different ways. For instance, caseworkers often felt inadequate and could potentially lose their jobs. Adolescent mothers faced homelessness and losing custody of their children as the possible costs of perceived noncompliance. We know the future is bleak for many young families transitioning from the child welfare system; however, we do not yet understand how youth needs are compromised by the same child welfare structures intended to foster the adolescent moms' success.

The young mothers (ages sixteen to twenty) with whom I worked lived alone with their children in apartments leased by a SIL program.[4] Federal, state, and local legislation provided the impetus for SIL, and the program was designed to prepare youth for "self-sufficient" adulthoods. Visions, a private nonprofit organization, ran this SIL program and supported fifty families in rented apartments at three buildings. Apartments were located in low-income, predominantly African American, urban communities in a large northeastern U.S. city. The SIL program in this book served a specific population of "aging out" youth: adolescent mothers and their young children. A judge ordered all placements. Two different branches of the child welfare system—the dependency program and the juvenile justice program—referred clients to SIL. The family court judged a youth to be a "dependent" of the state after authenticating that a caregiver had abused or neglected her. Such a youth would come under the jurisdiction of the dependency program. The family court judged a youth as "delinquent" for committing mainly nonviolent offenses, such as running away from home, drug possession, or petty theft. Such a youth would come under the jurisdiction of the juvenile justice program. The SIL program administered services the same way to both delinquent and dependent clients. Youth intermingled at the three community apartment sites were subject to the same program rules and received the same program resources and services. However, the child welfare and court systems treated delinquent youth more harshly than dependent youth, and delinquent youth received inequitable access to some resources such as childcare.

Youth coped with regulation in creative ways as they capably managed their identities, constructed informal support networks, and created impressions of compliance when actual compliance was infeasible. Simultaneously, youth had to prove themselves worthy of public care and capable of parenting. No matter how culturally resilient, young families experienced institutional and attitudinal barriers to their well-being. Foregrounding youth trajectories led to both losses and gains. My research did not elucidate elaborate constructions of particular system settings, but I believe that the benefits of this approach outweighed this loss; we gain a much-needed coherent narrative about youth identities.

Risky Critique

I realize that I take a risk in exposing these system challenges. In the United States, federal, state, and local governments are slashing social services, community programs, and public education for low-income youth of color (Tilton 2010). At the same time, more prisons are being built (Alexander 2012). Increased expenditure on U.S. penal systems is not indicative of a shift toward reduced government intervention in social life. Rather, the change indicates more exclusionary and punitive approaches to the regulation of marginalized communities (Davis 2003; Fisher and Reese 2011; Haney 2010). The SIL program, policies, and service negotiations described in this book must be understood in a situated historical and cultural context. Years have passed since the occurrence of the everyday interactions represented here, and many of the specific policies of SIL in this city have changed. I describe some of these changes in the conclusion, but many lessons about identity processes, discontinuities in power across system settings, and the role of grounded participant narratives remain pertinent. The quality of programming for youth in child welfare across the United States continues to be of concern to many clients, advocates, and officials (Courtney, Dworsky, and Napolitano 2013; Courtney and Dworsky 2006). Further, the disconnection and animosity between sectors of child welfare (legal, policy, and programming) continue to block collective efforts at improving services for children and youth.

In addition to the disconnection across public systems of governance—including child welfare, housing, health care, and childcare—this book also explores the unequal relationship between administrative and programmatic settings within the child welfare system. I show how these bureaucratic inequalities actually construct client "failure," and I shift the diagnosis of the problem from client attributes to system biases. I hope that this book will inspire conversations across diverse constituents. It should serve as one tool among others to reenvision governance systems, policies, and approaches that support the well-being of structurally disadvantaged youth and children. I do not want the book to be used to destroy the few public resources and services to which youth have access. Over and over, young mothers told me how the SIL program had saved their lives and how without it they would be either dead or locked up. I hope their portrayals chip away at a culture of fear and encourage better leverage of public and private resources.

Foreseeing the "Unforeseen" Implications of Child Welfare Policies

This book reveals the ways the child welfare system compromises its own mission and how it fails to alleviate hardship in the lives of young families. First, I demonstrate my findings that the child welfare system blocked youth from prospering through inequitable spatial divides between administrative settings and program spaces. Second, I bring into question the ideal of self-sufficiency and how it compelled youth and caseworkers to hide their structural insecurities. Third, I explore how conditions within the system caused a divisive culture of fear.

DISCONNECTED PROGRAM SETTINGS

I consider the different experiences of "street-level bureaucracy" among ground-level participants, including program managers, caseworkers, and clients (Lipsky 1980). Work conditions such as resource limitations, time pressures, and conflicting goals make it impossible for ground-level caseworkers to practice in ways that would meet official policies and ideals of care. Even though each group enacts "street-level" coping strategies, clients, caseworkers, and administrators form unique alliances and experience different expectations and stakes.

In SIL, inequalities between program settings and cumbersome bureaucratic procedures contributed to clients' and caseworkers' perceptions that upper-level administrators dictated rules without understanding the everyday lives of these clients and caseworkers. The state appeared to youth and caseworkers to be simultaneously everywhere and nowhere. Lynne Haney (2010) describes a contemporary neoliberal trend in which the government increasingly outsources public services to private for-profit or nonprofit organizations. Regulators use audits and documentation to oversee an agency's service provision. Even as government has "devolved, decentralized, and diversified" (Haney 2010: 15), many scholars argue that it has not shrunk. Haney (2010: 16) characterizes hybrid agencies of government as "akin to satellite states—they circle and hover around the centralized 'mother ship,' relying on her for material survival, legitimacy, and authority." In my study, multiple regulators oversaw each individual client's case, which caused clients to feel demoralized because they had little recourse for failed care. Clients were unable to determine which provider was responsible for which aspects of their care. Subsequently, the diffuse nature of governance meant that participants could not predict the repercussions for breaking the rules, which reinforced a culture of fear.

Upper-level SIL administrators included the financial officers, contract managers, grant writers, and directors who oversaw the SIL program and the other educational and residential programs offered by Visions. These upper-level administrators rarely if ever visited the SIL apartment sites. They occupied a "professional" business office with newly purchased furnishings and equipment. It was located in one of the city's wealthier and whiter suburbs, a forty-minute drive from the city's center. Most case managers were black women from the city, and most business office administrators were white women from the suburbs. Thus, the hierarchy within the agency mirrored and perpetuated the spatial, racial, and class-based divisions in the broader city.

Caseworkers struggled with how to oversee the "supervised" part of independent living because they worked in a hybrid environment. They did their jobs alongside the community members who lived in the apartment building and caseworkers had to deal with whatever violence or chaos this cohabitation created. Oversight was necessarily limited. Even though the official rules specified visiting hours and did not allow overnight visits, staff found it impossible to uphold these program rules. Before scheduled meetings with case managers, companions or family members could easily go from one apartment to another without being detected. Some youth would hide their visitors in their closets when they heard a knock at the door. Staff members were savvy to this tactic and would check closets or visit in pairs. One staff would knock on the apartment door and another would wait on the fire escape to catch the departing young man.

Staff did not universally uphold program rules. Some caseworkers broke rules for the more favored mothers. Or staff would give up the pretense of enforcing the no-visitor rule, accepting the reality that they could not control who entered and exited the community buildings. Some caseworkers found that their supervisors did not back up their efforts, so they stopped trying to follow the rules. Overall, many youth understood that certain staff members ignored the visitor policy, and their boyfriends and family members stayed with them in SIL apartments. The SIL program was disconnected spatially and bureaucratically from SIL administration, the Children and Youth Services (CYS) agency, and the court. Fragmentation caused delays in needed resources. But it also meant that the daily activities of program participants were invisible to supervisors and administrators.

SELF-SUFFICIENCY?

I watched as a female child-protection worker and two male police officers took a sixteen-year-old mother's child from her arms as the mom, Olivia, sat shaking and crying uncontrollably. Olivia's tear-stained face and closed eyes are forever imprinted in my memory. The officers' voices were soothing and gentle as they tried to comfort the teen. They waited patiently and allowed the mother to hold on and cry for a bit longer. I was a program manager at the time. This was a cross-agency decision, and Olivia's SIL case manager, CYS social worker, and I made the call together. The CYS worker arranged for the child's temporary placement.[5]

Removing Olivia's son from her care was the most difficult decision I made as a program manager. Olivia's son had burned himself while under her watch. Had this mother put her child's safety at risk? The answer was yes, according to the safety standards we were supposed to use. Yet I felt conflicted. The structure of the SIL program did not foster consistent guidance, a caring community, a safe environment, or a range of supports to help this mother parent her son. She lived alone with her son in a SIL apartment, and the rules prevented visitors from helping her care for her child. On her own, she was supposed to parent her son, go to high school, work part time, manage health-care appointments, attend court, and arrange for her son's childcare. One could argue that the program set her up to fail. I question whether the program's self-sufficiency expectations would be reasonable for any teenager (or, for that matter, any adult).

Olivia's situation was particularly dire. Although she needed a more supervised and structured residential option, such as a mother-and-baby group home, none was available. A placement in a mother-and-baby group home would have provided around-the-clock staff supervision and would have prevented us from separating

Olivia from her child. Unfortunately, the number of available spots in mother-and-baby placements in the child welfare system falls far short of the demand. Both the SIL program and the mother-and-baby group home had long waiting lists.

Olivia's identity as a mother was legally and morally questioned when "the system" took her son from her care. Officials put her in a position to prove her worthiness and to earn her ability to resume motherhood. In so many ways, officials pressed young mothers such as Olivia not only to justify their abilities as parents but also to earn their own care. Youth were forced to demonstrate personal worth in measurable ways—through benchmarks of self-sufficiency. Frequently, youth failed to meet these goals. In her position as a black, low-income, abused teen mother, the public and many others judged Olivia as unfit. Our misconceptions about who she was and who she could become cemented her low social position. Children burn themselves in middle-class homes, under the watch of married, adult mothers, and those children are not removed from their homes.[6] Olivia's actions were more scrutinized because she was a ward of the state. The individualized service plan averted our attention from all the ways we together constructed Olivia as a "failure." This was certainly not my intention, but, looking back, I see how I was an agent in this construction. Olivia was not alone. Unreasonable and undersupported expectations of self-sufficiency created impossible dilemmas for many youth and their caseworkers. The self-sufficiency myth reinforced a culture of fear in the program.

SUSTAINING A CULTURE OF FEAR

In SIL, alliances and resistances changed over time. On occasion, a client and caseworker would join in opposition to a program manager's order, or a client and program manager would resist a case manager's decision. In rare instances, mothers as a collective challenged their caseworker(s). On several occasions, youth and I resisted convoluted procedural protocols in order to obtain particular services. Sometimes clients would receive help from their probation officers, CYS workers, or judges in blocking the decisions of SIL staff members. These are just a few examples of the many types of shifting alliances. Many youth seemed to intuit or even strategize when resistance would be tolerated or when it would be in their best interests to perform sanctioned identities. The changing nature of governance meant that clients could not always predict appropriately, and sometimes they suffered severe consequences.

Lynne Haney (1996) identified separate private and public patriarchies in her comparison of a community-based probation program for delinquent adolescent girls and a publicly regulated group home for delinquent adolescent mothers. When the girls lived within their inner-city neighborhoods, they engaged in relationships with young men who subjected them to private patriarchy. By contrast, the patriarchy of the state maintained authority over the group home. I discovered a more nuanced relationship between public and private gender orders, which resisted a simply binary. Forms of power worked in relation to one another rather than through separate domains. Officially, the SIL program did not allow men at program sites; unofficially, it either ignored men or incorporated them into daily program life.

Power worked in complicated ways through a matrix of gender, class, race, and age divisions, even though it was conveyed through a fleeting "us versus them" dynamic. During formal audits, caseworkers and clients worked together to manage the impression of the men's absence. At other times, the authority of the staff and the men would conflict directly—when boyfriends abused clients or threatened staff. These men tended to be significantly older than the young women, and the men controlled the moms through economic and emotional leverage or through physical violence. Men asserted influence, even though they did not exist officially within the program.

For instance, one young mother dealt with friction between public and private patriarchies. Her "live-in" boyfriend threatened a maintenance worker as the worker conducted a routine repair. Officially, the boyfriend did not have authority over the worker. Yet a man with a gun need not respect the boundaries of the program's jurisdiction. After the incident, the SIL caseworker yelled at the mother, telling her it was her responsibility to stand up to her boyfriend. The worker told the client to gain control over her SIL apartment. I witnessed this interaction, the look of frustration, and the slow tears that trailed down the girl's face. She was stuck in an impossible situation, without the means to maintain power. This much older man victimized her repeatedly, and the situation was complicated by the fact that he was the father of her two young children.

Both governance and private oppressions created a diffuse sense of threat and fear. Youth lived in this fractured and unjust world, in which SIL program spaces intersected with wider oppressions. These intersections did not liberate, but rather confined, their bodies and actions. While important, it simply is not enough to provide a roof over a young family's head with access to some basic resources. A pervasive culture of fear hindered open identity explorations and collective problem solving. Participants' accounts point to an urgent need to reenvision and improve systems of care.

Origin, Methods, and Critical Standpoints

RESEARCHER-ADVOCATE

My subjectivities influenced this account, and I reveal myself as a player throughout the book. I used my own standpoint as a window into the SIL program. My identity as an ethnographer was multifaceted, as I had worked for SIL for two years before conducting the research. Differences in power shaped how I made sense of my roles and the social world I encountered in the system. After I had completed my master's degree, SIL hired me as a program manager. I was a white, middle-class woman in my late twenties at the time. I had written my ethnographic master's thesis about young families who lived in a child welfare-supported group home. I had never worked in social services, and all of a sudden I was a supervisor of a staff composed of black female caseworkers and black male maintenance workers. Several staff members were older than I was and had worked in the field for many years. I had a master's degree but very little practical experience. I often felt uncomfortable, especially with what I represented to my staff. During these moments, my supervisor (white, middle aged, and female) reminded me of the reason she had hired me. Purportedly I possessed something that could not be taught: a strong sense of compassion for the girls. She believed that she could teach me everything else about how to run a program. But could she teach me how to address the staff's bitterness and reasonable sense of injustice? How would I deal with staff challenges to my leadership as I struggled to build partnerships and connect with the youth? Through these tensions, I became more cognizant of the racial, economic, spatial, and educational divides that shaped our practices and my role.

As a SIL program manager, I was an individual with relative power, and I was responsible for the young families and my staff. Even as an official agent, I was unable to fulfill our mission of protecting adolescents and their children and of helping mothers to complete their education and become independent. I conducted ethnographic fieldwork because I wanted to understand why I was ineffective, the injustices I witnessed, and the unmet aspirations of young mothers.

As a practitioner, I too felt trapped in "the system," which many of us (both clients and officials) blamed for what was wrong with governance. We gave the system agency, personifying it as something both above us and encompassing us (Ferguson and Gupta 2002). The concept became a catchall for an intangible amalgam of power inequities, multiple public institutions, and convoluted procedural protocols—a messy and unpredictable web within which our bodies, choices, and movements felt constrained. I wanted to do as Dorothy Smith (2008), a feminist sociologist who pioneered institutional ethnography, would have suggested: reclaim and bring attention to the actions of youth and practitioners in the making of SIL and other institutional relations. When practitioners, policymakers, and clients conceive of institutions as patterns produced by procedures but not by people, we transfer agency to "the system" and away from us, the social actors. In contrast, Smith asks researchers to construct knowledge through contextualizing and demythologizing institutional patterns (Smith 2008; Sprague 2005). Through participants' perspectives, we can begin to see taken-for-granted "translocal" (Smith 2008: 420) power relations that organize daily, local activities.

Once I started the research, I continued to advocate for young families across many service negotiations. This was a political, ethical, and practical decision for me. Caseworkers were overburdened with high caseloads, and youth could go several months without a caseworker. I both possessed situated bureaucratic knowledge and did not want to act like an "objective" observer if this meant that a young family would not receive a particular service. I tended to step in and assist, and I interpreted the contexts for my own decision making as well as its effects. Advocacy contributed to my research goals because I wanted to understand how participants created the system and reconstituted polices on the ground. My presence changed the social landscape, and my research shifted over time in response to the relational needs of my participants (Pillow and Mayo 2012).

My decision to advocate, as an integrated part of my research, can be conceived through a broad methodological lens. Anthropologists have always engaged in various forms of advocacy (whether explicit or implicit), and even deciding against action has political and practical implications (Rylko-Bauer, Singer, and Van Willigen 2006). Roger Sanjek (2004: 447) elucidates two connections between research and advocacy. First, he notes that "for some anthropologists advocacy occurs mainly during fieldwork, with advocacy goals determining research practice." Second, he explains that for others, advocacy takes place beyond the research setting when scholars engage public audiences. My approach aligns with Sanjek's dual characterizations, and I seek to use my book as a tool to engage public audiences. I agree with Victor Rios (2011: 16), who suggests that "helping people and generating solid empirical research are not mutually exclusive."

I felt more effective as a researcher-advocate than I ever did as program manager. I experienced freedom to help with whatever my participants needed at the time, and since I was no longer in a position of authority, staff members were amenable to my new role, even seeking out my assistance. The chapters that follow are drawn from the data I collected during my research phase, which took place from January 2003 through February 2005. In addition to how my role as researcher-advocate affected my approach, my experiences as a program manager shaped my orientation to the program and its clients. Several of the participants in the research were youth or staff members I had worked with as a program manager.

I chose to shadow clients across SIL sites, health-care clinics, schools, job-training sites, public housing offices, childcare settings, and courtrooms. This approach offered insight into both formal and informal practices. I, like other critical youth ethnographers, used shadowing to understand the ways youth performed and shifted their identities across time and myriad settings (see, e.g., Jones 2010; Nolan 2011; and Rios 2011). Shadowing elucidated the situated and constructed nature of taken-for-granted institutional discourses concerning the so-called irresponsible teen mom, the damaged dependent child, and the duplicitous delinquent youth.

I did extensive fieldwork within specific SIL contexts because I wanted to understand the central role of this child welfare program in the young families' lives. The bulk of my fieldwork took place at the largest SIL site, Evergreen Apartments, even though I spent time observing at all three residential sites. I experienced administrative and program divides by conducting some fieldwork at the urban SIL administrative office and the suburban Visions business office.[7] I participated in countless conversations and a select range of recorded, open-ended qualitative interviews with youth at each of the three SIL residential sites, with SIL staff members, and with a few upper-level administrators in the local Children and Youth Services agency and court system.[8]

CRITICAL STANDPOINTS

Feminist methodology and critical youth studies informed how I asked questions, how I approached my fieldwork, how I understood participants' and my own subjectivities, and the purpose of this account. This book, like other feminist ethnographies, privileges three objectives: (1) analyzing gender in the context of constructions of race, class, and sexuality; (2) using research for social change; and (3) exploring researcher reflexivity (Pillow and Mayo 2012).

Feminist scholars resist conceptualizing social realities as the results of individual choices. Instead, they look through multiple standpoints, which are created through intersecting inequalities of race, gender, class, and sexuality (Collins 2000; Crenshaw 1995; Harris 2000; Razack 1998). Standpoints construct different versions of knowledge as "partial, local, and historically specific" (Sprague

2005: 41). One's access to material, cultural, and social resources shapes one's standpoint. Standpoint theorists resist analyzing a "problem" such as youth delinquency or teen parenthood as an individual choice and instead explain how the social order makes the "problem" likely (Rios 2011; Sprague 2005). Yet feminists have undertheorized age constructions as intersections with gender (Miller 2006). This book, then, adds to the body of feminist ethnography through centering the lives of marginalized *young* women. Social constructions of children and youth affect the nature of child welfare policies and officials' interpretations of the policies. Age constructions are an important aspect of both identity and power, and I examine how youth categories (legal and social) shape the standpoints of young mothers in a SIL program, as well as the nature of the services they receive. Even as understandings of the social world are always partial, more inclusive and nuanced versions pay attention to patterns, connections, and fragmentation across multiple standpoints. This book, while focused on young mothers, draws from the unique viewpoints of different participants in child welfare, including caseworkers, administrative officials, and myself.

In additional to feminist ethnography, I draw on critical youth studies. Scholarly attention to children and youth has a long history. As a multidisciplinary field, childhood studies, which includes the study of youth, is a new and expanding endeavor. Insights from the fields of anthropology, sociology, and psychology, when combined, reveal children and youth to be complex, intentional, and resilient actors. In particular, youth negotiate state regulation through gender, age, sexuality, and race constructions, as well as through diverse institutional and social contexts. In her introduction to *Children and the Politics of Culture*, Sharon Stephens (1995) notes a key tension that scholars today continue to address: while conceptions of protected, "normative" childhoods expand globally, so do punitive discourses and policies for addressing so-called out-of-place children (see, e.g., Bluebond-Langner and Korbin 2007; Korbin and Anderson-Fye 2011; Nolan 2011; Jones 2010; Rios 2011; and Tilton 2010).

I join other critical youth ethnographers Victor Rios (2011), Nikki Jones (2010), and Kathleen Nolan (2011), who work from the assumption that youth participants, marginalized through categories of race and class, are "normal." Youth behaviors make sense as survival strategies in urban contexts of extreme structural disadvantage (racism, poverty, and gender oppression). These youth, like all of us, attempt to safeguard their dignity and nurture their livelihoods as they cope in treacherous, punitive, and unjust environments. Critical youth scholars critique dichotomous representations, neither glamorizing youth as heroes and heroines nor distorting their agency as victims (Rios 2011). I represent the complex, creative, changing, and contradictory standpoints of young people in the child welfare system. Taking a broad interdisciplinary approach, this book ultimately calls for changes in child welfare and in the care of marginalized children and youth more generally.

Chapter Summaries

Chapter 1 describes the inequalities between program settings, including SIL apartment sites, the SIL administrative office, and the private agency's business office. The agencies required case managers to provide comprehensive services and to document these. Caseworkers explained to me that public expectations were unrealistic because of the *actual* realities of the job. Case managers felt discounted by administrative supervisors and inauthentic in their positions. Faith, a case manager, complained that she did not receive the resources necessary to do her job, as she referred to the "broken junk" in her apartment office and the filing cabinets that were "busted" and did not lock. She wondered whether administrators considered how caseworkers felt when visiting the professional-looking business office. If the conditions of her workspace were more professional, she said, she would not feel like she was "playing case manager." I explain the work experiences of case managers to show structurally why so many of them were unable to provide comprehensive care to their clients.

Chapter 2 considers how youth, and their case managers, coped in underresourced, dangerous SIL residential settings. To meet personal needs and create the impression of compliance, participants used a "zone of familiar ease" (Herzfeld 2005: 372). *Familiar zones* formed at program sites because of the social and physical distance from administrative sites. Participants used familiar zones to hide aspects of program life (such as live-in boyfriends and violence) that conflicted with official expectations. One woman, Tomeka, used the program's GED classroom as a familiar zone. She complied with the judge's requirement that she attend an educational program. Invisible to the judge was the fact that Tomeka and several other SIL participants brought their babies with them to class (because they did not receive childcare services). The familiar zone hid the childcare duties that took place in the educational setting, which, of course, compromised GED preparation. In other instances, participants broke program rules, often doing so out of necessity and because social realities did not match official descriptions. The chapter explores the creative ways mothers and case managers coped in program familiar zones. On the other hand, because oversight did not extend to familiar zones, these spaces tended to perpetuate oppressive conditions, including violence and neglect.

Chapter 3 looks closely at how young mothers presented their identities during official negotiations. Youth were aware of the need to appear worthy of public investment and capable of self-reform. Particularly when clients were afraid of being discharged, they attempted to align their identities with official expectations. Through several vignettes, I explore the perceptiveness of young mothers in this process. Ideologies of self-sufficiency complicated and compromised open, flexible, and fluid identities. When making discharge decisions, caseworkers would discuss a client's disposition. However, these evaluations were secondary to considerations about risk. Kelley, a nineteen-year-old mother, was in danger of being discharged from the program because of the men (perceived to be drug dealers) she interacted with in her SIL apartment. Desperate to remain in the SIL program in order to regain custody of her daughter, she presented herself and was perceived by SIL staff as a hard worker and a respectful client. Her weakness, as one staff member suggested, was in the "man field." Kelley struggled with contradictory discursive expectations. On the one hand, Kelley had to embody victimization and appear like a youth who deserved and needed services. On the other hand, Kelley had to demonstrate that she was capable of making responsible decisions. The divide between victim and self-efficacious identities was a tenuous one, putting Kelley in an impossible situation. This chapter looks briefly outside the child welfare system and elucidates a paradox in self-sufficiency rhetoric. A job-training program prepared young females for the lowest rungs of the U.S. service economy.

Chapter 4 introduces a case study as I highlight my advocacy with one young mother, Nyisha. Together, we negotiated housing with officials from the Public Housing Authority. At the time, Nyisha was approaching her twenty-first birthday, at which point she would age out of the child welfare system. A close look at this case provides an opportunity to explain how shifting cultural and organizational contexts shaped our strategies. Material deficits, spatial barriers, and bureaucratic procedures restricted the story lines clients and officials used to make sense of one another. Youth performed their identities according to system-sanctioned expectations (i.e., as deserving victims) because successful negotiations were essential to receiving services. In this instance, Nyisha felt compelled to reveal her identity as a rape survivor in order to justify access to a safe residence.

Not only did mothers manage impressions by enacting acceptable narratives around program compliance; sometimes they engaged in everyday acts of resistance. Chapter 5 expands on examples of resistance explored in prior chapters. In the chapter I define and demonstrate a range of individual and collective resistances. Most often, clients rebelled in program familiar zones, where they believed they would likely avoid punishment. Sometimes, confrontation escalated and backfired against particular clients. In one case, a CYS worker ignored the official procedures involved in taking under custody a client's child. The client was so distraught that she hit her SIL program manager, and charges were brought against the youth. The mother had little recourse against the CYS worker's unreasonable discretion to take her child away, and her resistance appeared to stem from helplessness and rage. The chapter demonstrates how unpredictable repercussions and shifting alliances contributed to a divisive ethos of blame among participants.

In the conclusion, I provide an update on the federal, state, and local legislative landscape concerning SIL and services for youth in care. Finally, I propose some ideas for innovating SIL. We need to foster grassroots participation and social inclusion at all levels of government. Without adequate government support, marginalized adolescent mothers and their children are susceptible to greater hardship, and hence it is vital that the institutions and programs in place be reformed justly (not eliminated).

CHAPTER ONE

Playing Case Manager

Work Life in a Culture of Fear

On many occasions, caseworkers articulated their common belief that program managers and business office administrators did not understand their experiences "on the ground" and that supervisors did not care about caseworker job realities. While program managers had more access to SIL residential environments, the administrators at the business office rarely, if ever, visited apartment sites. As Rachelle, a case manager, told me in regard to business office administrators,

> They don't even know their way to my site. . . . I have a problem with that. They don't understand. . . . They sit in the office and dictate what should be happening, but they don't come down here for the reality part.

Rachelle referred to the social distance created as those in power dictated bureaucratic procedures while not experiencing or understanding the "reality" of SIL environments.

Rachelle was the only caseworker at the Chatham apartment site, which housed twenty-three young families. She was African American and in her early thirties at the time of our interview. Rachelle became a mother when she was a teenager, and her experiences as a teen mom guided her interactions with the young families. For four months, she had been the lone caseworker at this building and was responsible for managing both her own caseload and clients from the absent worker's caseload. The agency's difficulty retaining staff increased Rachelle's burden. She was tasked with managing a caseload in excess of the ten-client maximum stated in the SIL program manual.

Discrepancies in program environments contributed to a sense of social and status difference between administrators and program managers, on the one hand, and between administrators and case managers, on the other. Differences between physical environments and the distance between program city sites and the suburban business office mapped distinctions in value across the organization. Also, case managers did not have access to the tools and technology necessary for doing their jobs. The agency supplied their offices with secondhand furniture and equipment. Administrators occupied a newly furnished and well-equipped suburban office. Caseworkers interpreted these differences to mean that the organization undervalued them. Moving across program sites, I experienced these inequalities, as well as the standpoints of participants in these contexts (Sprague 2005). This book contextualizes the narratives of mothers and their caseworkers as together they negotiated identities and services across bureaucratic settings. Even moms who liked and enjoyed their case managers would talk about the general ineffectiveness of these same caseworkers. In this chapter, I focus on the SIL staff's work experiences to explain the structures and environments that compromised their interactions with clients and their capacities to assist. First, I provide necessary background on SIL policies and programming, the SIL governance structure, and multiple settings in the program.

Systems of SIL

SIL POLICIES AND PROGRAM DESCRIPTIONS

Wendy Smith (2011) notes that policies and research focused almost entirely on young children in the child welfare system until the 1980s, when the public recognized that older youth in care needed assistance transitioning to adulthood. As she explains, "The Independent Living Program was initially enacted through the Title IV-E of the Social Security Act of 1985 (PL 99–272) and was augmented through the Foster Care Independence Act (FCIA) of 1999, when it became known as the Chafee Foster Care Independent Living Program" (213). This federal legislation allowed youth between the ages of sixteen and eighteen to receive transitional services. Youth stopped receiving assistance when they aged out of child welfare on their eighteenth birthdays. The most recent bill, the Fostering Connections to Success and Increasing Adoptions Act of 2008, gave states the *option* to provide services to youth in foster care until the age of twenty-one.[1] Before this bill was passed in 2008—and before I conducted my research—the city, which housed the SIL program, had implemented its own policy, which extended care to the age of twenty-one. Extended assistance was contingent on whether a youth participated in an educational program. As we will see in the following chapters, officials did not consistently apply this stipulation. The local CYS discharged many youth before their twenty-first birthdays. Even the fear of potential discharge contributed to a culture of threat within the SIL program.

The child welfare system prioritizes reuniting children with their families or adoption. These emphases mean that most young children in foster care exit long before they become eligible for independent living services. Therefore, most participants in SIL became wards of the state during their adolescence. Because CYS funded 85 percent of the total cost to run SIL, the program aligned with public priorities.[2] State and federal governments mandated CYS to protect the well-being of court-ordered dependent and delinquent youth. Young mothers maintained custody of their own children unless CYS substantiated cause to take the children under its jurisdiction.

Clients received program resources that included a weekly stipend, an apartment (equipped with secondhand furniture), toiletries, diapers, cleaning supplies, a public transportation pass, and medical assistance. However, SIL did not provide these resources unconditionally. For youth to receive program services, they were required by a network of providers to participate in school, work part time, care for their children, and attend routine court hearings. In addition, many were court-ordered to attend supplemental programs, including parenting classes, anger management classes, psychotherapy, and drug and alcohol rehabilitation programs.

GOVERNANCE

CYS contracted the SIL program to provide services to young families, and its oversight was implemented through two mechanisms.

First, both the state and CYS separately audited the SIL program once a year, visiting SIL sites to inspect for safety, review case files, and interview staff. Seemingly objective inspections were supposed to determine whether the SIL program met the standards of care that it claimed to address. Second, an official from the referring public agency supervised each client. The city mandated that CYS workers meet with each dependent client on their caseloads at least once every six months. A judge assigned a juvenile probation officer (PO) to monitor each delinquent youth's behavior in the community. CYS workers, POs, SIL case managers, and clients together attended routine court hearings, during which the judge would review the client's residential placement in SIL.

An Individual Service Plan (ISP), presumably created in cooperation between the SIL case manager, the CYS worker (or PO), and the young mother, documented (in six-month intervals) goals for youth development as well as the outcomes and challenges in meeting the previously established goals. However, youth did not tend to be equal partners in developing their ISPs. Case managers and other providers dictated essential areas for life-skills development, education, or social "rehabilitation." Within these stipulations, youth could sometimes choose which programs they would like to attend. Nevertheless, they faced barriers in their educational and occupational decision making. Lack of childcare, health problems, and domestic violence often limited youth from participating in their education and professional development. Further, within this underresourced, racially segregated urban area, quality public educational programs were hard to find. In addition to supplying ISPs, SIL case managers involved CYS workers or POs when clients were discharged from the program. Thus, CYS workers and POs did not actively engage in a mother's day-to-day life; these responsibilities fell primarily to the SIL case managers.

The SIL program was staffed by a variety of employees who performed diverse tasks, among them case management, program management, safety monitoring, administrative assistance, and apartment maintenance. Given the range of staff required to run the SIL program, I focus primarily on case managers and program managers,[3] as their decisions and actions most readily shaped youth experiences of services in the SIL program. The program managers both supervised case managers and were responsible for the overall operation of the SIL program. The residential director oversaw all the residential programs offered by the wider agency, including the SIL program. (Throughout, I refer to the holder of this position as the "SIL program director"). Visions agency provided a number of residential, educational, and advocacy programs to women and children. In this book, I investigate the nested relationships within the SIL program.

Case managers were responsible for all the daily activities involved in providing services and regulating clients and their children. The case managers worked from apartments in the same buildings that housed the SIL participants. The worker apartments were transformed into offices with phones, fax machines, computers, and secondhand desks. Each case manager was supposed to carry a maximum caseload of ten young mothers and their children. The official responsibilities of the case manager job were threefold: (1) caseworkers administered services or coordinated them with outside providers in the areas of health care, schooling, parenting education, employment, life skills, household management, legal services, and counseling; (2) caseworkers regulated mothers, making sure they adhered to the rules of the program and fulfilled their obligations as residents, mothers, students, and employees; and (3) caseworkers completed mandated reports and documented in case notes all services provided by the SIL program and external agencies.

The multifaceted areas of case management established the comprehensive nature of the position: "Case management involves coordinating all services necessary to allow the client and her children to achieve maximum personal growth and self sufficiency. . . . The SIL case manager wears many hats and plays many roles including counselor, surrogate parent, teacher, hand holder, enabler, and mentor" (excerpt from program manual).

Across localities, low salaries, unreasonable caseload expectations, and insufficient training have led to very high turnover rates for child welfare workers (CLASP 2004). First, at the most basic level, high turnover challenges the formation of consistent and meaningful relationships between adults and youth (Freundlich and Avery 2005). Second, officials do not usually entrust youth to navigate services, such as health care, childcare, and psychological services, on their own behalf; clients rely on the advocacy of their case managers. Third, high turnover means that clients and young families often do not have available case managers to help them navigate services.

High turnover in SIL meant that case managers often did not have the program- or case-specific knowledge to successfully support their clients. It was common for youth in the SIL program to go several months without a SIL case manager. In the interim, other SIL caseworkers or program managers would oversee the cases. This was not seamless. "Cases," or young families, would slip through the cracks, because already overtaxed caseworkers and program managers would not meet the comprehensive mandates described above.

The program manager role was diversified across areas of administration, staff supervision, and client care. Program managers were responsible for supervising and training their case managers. They were in charge of conducting intake interviews to evaluate a potential client and to prepare a plan to address any underlying psychological or behavioral concerns. Program managers found it extremely difficult to retain qualified staff, and they filled gaps as needed. Often, this included engaging in case management, delivering supplies, picking up vouchers for client clothing, babysitting, providing counseling, and taking youth to doctor's appointments or grocery shopping. The program managers worked from a SIL administrative office, also furnished with secondhand items and located in the inner city, but in a different locale from the apartments. This building housed an agency GED program, which many of the SIL clients attended.

Upper-level administrators included the financial officers, contract managers, grant writers, and agency directors who oversaw the SIL program and all other programs offered by Visions. Upper-level agency administrators occupied a business office located in the suburbs. The SIL director resided in this office. Officially, the director was not in charge of daily supervision and staff training for SIL.

However, when I initiated fieldwork, the director was involved in these matters because both the program managers were new hires; as my fieldwork concluded, she was providing oversight because both program managers had quit.

As I have noted, the spatialization of status was also racialized, as mostly white, female administrators worked from the suburban business office and mostly black, female case managers and clients occupied sites within low-income sections of the city. Young moms and their case managers described their environments as unsafe and threatening, particularly as drug trafficking and the dangers associated with it infiltrated the program settings. My interactions with youth, children, and their caseworkers took place through the interface between these unique and fragmented SIL program environments.

Everyday Journey across SIL Spaces

I share the events described here as a way to mark and elucidate the salient case management and environmental challenges that were common in the program. I will return to these issues and explore them in more detail throughout the book.

One morning I arrived at the SIL administrative office. After chatting with Ms. Rose, the administrative assistant, with whom I had worked when I was on staff, I accepted the invitation of Teresa, a recently hired SIL program manager, to have coffee at the newly opened café across the street. I had introduced myself to Teresa a few days earlier and explained my research as well as my prior role as a SIL program manager.

The SIL administrative office was located in a converted row home on a block with several abandoned houses, kitty-corner from a small shopping center with a hair salon and local shops that appeared to cater to a mainly African American clientele. Ethiopian immigrants ran the café across the street, and it was a peaceful sanctuary with earth-toned walls covered in African art and fabrics. The SIL administrative office was located in an inner-city, mixed residential and commercial neighborhood. Because of its close proximity to a university, the neighborhood was slowly starting to gentrify.

Building renovations were underway, and students with backpacks could be seen walking the streets.

Teresa was a middle-aged African American woman who had worked in the local juvenile justice system before joining the SIL-providing agency. I welcomed her offer to join her for coffee, and as we sat sipping our drinks at the café, Teresa expressed her desire to hear about my prior experiences as a SIL program manager. She ended up doing most of the talking and appeared to feel relief while unloading her frustrations. Teresa began by expressing what a difficult time she was having with the job, which she said she had almost quit several times. Little of the work she had done was in her job description. In fact, she spent most of her time doing the caseworkers' jobs. She was frustrated with her case managers, who she said didn't work, couldn't write case notes properly, and would spend sixty minutes talking about mundane issues, such as a client's cat. Although I suggested that the caseworkers might feel overwhelmed and undertrained, as she did, she replied that she simply needed different caseworkers. The program's focus was backward, according to Teresa, as it expected clients to meet a wide range of performance outcomes without sufficiently helping them to address underlying repercussions of abuse.

After returning to the SIL administrative office with Teresa, I greeted Helen, a long-standing SIL worker, who was about to leave for Evergreen, the apartment building that housed the most SIL families. Over the weekend there had been a domestic fight and a client's boyfriend had destroyed the client's refrigerator. Helen was leaving to investigate. African American and middle aged, Helen was a nurturing, motherly figure to many staff members and clients. It was common for prior clients to return to SIL after many years to visit and chat with Helen. As she did not have a college degree, she was unable to hold a case management position, yet she was known around SIL as a "jack of all trades." I knew Helen well because I had been her supervisor and we had worked together closely. I welcomed the opportunity to accompany her to Evergreen.

Evergreen was located a brief drive from the SIL administrative office. A short walk from the apartment building was a small shopping area with a supermarket, a dollar store, and a seafood takeout.

When we arrived, Helen realized that she no longer had access, as a security system had been installed. She had given her only electric key to a SIL resident who had just moved in with a new baby. Helen had been waiting for several weeks for the delayed check to purchase more keys from the landlord. The check would be issued from the agency's suburban business office. To complicate matters, the buzzer for the SIL staff office did not work. She began ringing various other apartments leased by the SIL program, to no avail. Finally, an unknown person walked out and we slipped in.

I noticed that the expansive front hall was newly painted beige; the area felt brighter than I had remembered. The elevator looked exactly the same. It was old-fashioned, with an iron gate that banged loudly, and it had layers of filth covering the inside. I recalled a supervisor's once telling me that in the 1920s this building had been an upscale hotel. Now dirty and rickety, the elevator seemed like a remnant from this past. The patchwork of hallways in this four-story building seemed to be in transition, some newly covered in gray or blue carpet. The décor was mismatched. Other hallways had the old carpeting or linoleum flooring, stained in various places. The lighting was uneven, with some floors well lit while the dimness of others inspired apprehension.

We took the elevator to the office on the top floor, where Rebecca, a caseworker hired a month before, was occupied at her desk. Helen used one of her personal keys to unlock a filing cabinet, which stored the master set of SIL apartment keys. The SIL caseworkers had access to all clients' apartments at any time of day, signifying the authority of the regulatory agency. Rebecca, who was white and in her mid-twenties, remarked that she would come along with us to check the damaged apartment.

With each step Helen took, the wide ring of keys jingled, announcing our arrival long before the knock on a client's door. We approached the apartment where the domestic dispute had reportedly occurred. Helen knocked, received no answer, and then unlocked the door. We entered and I noticed a pile of broken glass in front of the inside door. Helen examined the refrigerator. I was startled as the bedroom door creaked open and a young man walked out, blinking and rubbing his eyes. He was wearing only boxer shorts.

Rebecca asked him where the mom was. He responded that she had gone to school, adding that his kids were asleep in the bedroom. There was an awkward silence following his remarks. As we were leaving, Helen instructed him to clean up the glass, which was hazardous for the kids. After we entered the hallway, I asked Helen if that was the boyfriend who had caused the damage and she said yes, adding in a cynical tone that boyfriends were now allowed to babysit in the apartments while moms attended school. Officially, it was against program rules for a nonresident to be in a SIL apartment outside of visiting hours.

After returning to the office, Helen complained about how things around the program had changed, repeatedly saying that caseworkers were overworked, ignored, and without any real control. The case managers' decisions were never followed and were consistently overridden by the program managers. According to Helen, frequent emergencies and a caseload spread across multiple locations interrupted completion of case management. Also, caseworkers dealt with mandates to frequently appear in court with one client or another. In fact, Nel, the other case manager who worked from this site, was at court with a client that very morning. I asked Rebecca whether she agreed with Helen. She did not directly answer the question, saying instead that she was unclear about her boundaries and her role as a case manager. We continued to chat while Helen and Rebecca engaged in various tasks. Helen repeatedly mentioned the unsafe environment in the building, despite renovations. She lamented the number of drug dealers involved with the girls in the program and posited that some of the moms were also dealing drugs. Helen feared for the safety of program participants, SIL staff, and herself. She regretted the wide availability of guns, relatively absent when she had first started working for the program many years earlier.

Over the course of the next couple of hours, the office took on the general hustle and bustle characteristic of this space. Caseworkers grew adept at multitasking as they fielded calls from program managers, business office administrators, CYS workers, probation officers, and clients. They also tried to complete paperwork while chatting and meeting with clients. Moms and kids circulated through the office to make requests, report faulty equipment, use a computer or a telephone, or simply chat with the staff. The maintenance men visited often to eat their lunches, hang out with caseworkers, or make phone calls. The apartment offices were particularly cluttered because they served as storage locations for client supplies and toiletries. The maintenance men also stored small furnishings in the office. The noise level was almost always elevated: one worker might be conversing with a mother while another would be on the phone with the business office and a couple of the maintenance men would be joking around with the girls. The mood was generally jovial and upbeat, although case managers also complained that it was impossible to complete paperwork there. On many occasions, I witnessed the mood plummet abruptly as a youth (or sometimes a worker) erupted in frustration about unmet requests or services.

For instance, on that particular morning, Khadisha, one of the young SIL mothers, entered the office with her two young children. Helen and Rebecca exclaimed, "What are you wearing?!" Khadisha had a towel wrapped around her waist (she insisted that she had "booty" shorts on underneath). She explained that she had covered herself in the hallway to discourage the drug dealers from looking at her. The caseworkers insisted that the towel around Khadisha's waist didn't create a better image. Helen was interrupted by a phone call from the agency's suburban business office. After hanging up, she told us it was a request for a list of clients, children, and clients' status as either adjudicated dependents or delinquents. Helen and the staff had already provided the business office with this information, but the business office had lost it and was bothering caseworkers to look it up again. "And they wonder why we don't get everything done."

Rebecca informed Khadisha about a new high school that had just opened downtown for older students who had earned fewer than three credits. After fielding Khadisha's frustration—Khadisha had already paid for a GED program at the local community college—Rebecca suggested she could try to get reimbursed, since she had not started yet. At this point in the conversation, Khadisha's friend Donique walked into the office with her two-year-old son. Rebecca made the same suggestion about the high school to Donique, who angrily asserted, "I don't hear anyone talking about childcare!" She, along with Khadisha and the children, brusquely left the office. The rest of us were quiet for a few moments and then Rebecca offered, "She's right. If the girls are told they must be in school or else they will be forced to leave the program, then they must be given childcare. It's a basic requirement." Helen and I agreed. The juvenile justice program placed both Donique and Khadisha in SIL, and as a result of their status as delinquents they were not entitled to receive childcare through CYS. In contrast, dependent mothers received childcare directly through CYS.

Another young mom entered the office and asked for her weekly stipend check. Rebecca told her to return after 3:00 P.M., when they would be giving out the checks. This was in accordance with the program's policy, as girls were supposed to be in school and therefore could not retrieve their checks before three o'clock. Young women had been coming in and out of the office, clearly not attending school. Then the office cleared out and became quieter as Helen traveled to another SIL site to meet with a client. Rebecca told me she felt overwhelmed by her job. Her program managers didn't listen, and administrators didn't understand the needs of the girls or the nature of the caseworker job. She continued to suggest that the program managers enabled the girls to be treated like adults, meaning the girls could get away with absolutely anything, while the caseworkers had no power because administrators didn't support their decisions. Rebecca raised the pitch of her voice to imitate one of the program managers: "Oh, why do the girls hang out with the drug dealers?" In her own voice Rebecca answered, "Well, they need money and protection, so of course they'll hang out with the guys." Her tone became more subdued as she acknowledged that the girls were not safe living here.

These discussions took place with SIL staff as we interacted with several youth and children. Caseworkers bemoaned the dangerous work conditions they faced and the living conditions endured by the girls. Caseworkers referred to the implications of social distance as they talked about the ways their supervisors held them to unrealistic expectations and did not support them in upholding consequences for client "misbehavior." They felt that program managers did not fully understand caseworker realities or support caseworkers' decisions. Meanwhile, a program manager was frustrated with what she perceived as the inability of her case managers to do their jobs. Furthermore, social distance was cemented, since caseworkers, program managers, and business office administrators did not work from the same locales and therefore did not have common program experiences. Paperwork would get lost in the transfer across settings, and case managers would be asked to recompile documentation they had already submitted. This was a very common occurrence. Interestingly, both case managers and the program manager felt uncertain about their roles. They revealed a sense of disorder while they coped in dangerous and underresourced SIL sites. Donique and Khadisha, young delinquent mothers, despaired about the lack of staff attention to childcare. Rebecca presented an educational "option" that was infeasible because the program did not also provide daycare. This interaction points to the gap between program expectations and program supports. I explore these disparities further in chapter 2.

While top-level administrators tended to remain spatially and socially separate from clients and apartment sites, SIL case managers were highly mobile. They worked and interacted with clients at the apartment buildings. They periodically visited the business office for meetings and other types of communication. They thus witnessed and experienced the spatial divide. Over the course of a Monday morning, SIL staff and I traversed several program spaces.

I began that morning at the SIL administrative office, where I spoke to a program manager and an administrative assistant. The SIL administrative office was distinct from the apartment sites, but it was also located in a relatively low-income area of the city. Then I spent time in the on-site office with Helen, Rebecca, and a number of clients. Nel, the other newly hired site case manager, was at court for a routine client judicial review. Late in the morning, Helen traveled again to meet with a client at a different SIL apartment site. On any given day, it was typical for a caseworker to move across several program contexts. Caseworkers noted that constant traveling across disparate sites compromised their ability to complete all required case management tasks, including paperwork. Their time became fractured across multiple settings and cases.[4]

Rachelle described the challenging nature of her job; she served clients at multiple program locations on any given day. On Mondays, she attended a staff meeting at the SIL administrative office, yet she also needed to be at her apartment site to hand out weekly client stipend checks.[5] SIL policy required that the girls pick up their checks after 3:00 P. M., but since she was the lone site worker and had multiple responsibilities (including attending the meeting), Rachelle gave checks out earlier in the day. For girls she did not see, she left checks with notes in their apartments. Even as her practice went against program policy, her resourcefulness enabled her to meet all expectations: the young families received their weekly stipends, and she was able to attend the meeting.

"Playing Case Manager"

Case managers were required to offer comprehensive services, including practices of documentation. As caseworkers noted in the narrative that opened this chapter, these extensive expectations were unrealistic in light of the job realities. Work conditions shaped how caseworkers felt about themselves in their positions, as well as about supervisors and clients. It is essential to consider the standpoints of case managers so that we can better understand the conditions that hindered their ability to form fruitful relationships with clients.

During a Monday staff meeting, Faith, a case manager, complained that she did not receive the resources necessary to do her job. The agency had recently hired Faith to join Rachelle at the Chatham apartment building. Faith described the "broken junk" in her apartment office and the filing cabinets that were "busted" and did not lock. She wondered whether administrators considered how caseworkers felt when visiting the business office, which looked like a professional office. If the conditions of her workspace were more professional, she would not feel like she was "playing case manager." The mapping of hierarchy within the agency across economic status, race, and suburban/urban locale linked with intangible qualities of professionalism, personal value, and happiness.

Roberta Iversen (2004: 128) suggests that the definition of *profession* remains vague: "Professionals have characteristically claimed the right to a high degree of autonomy, established and sustained by privileged, if not monopolistic, practices and exclusionary regulatory mechanisms." Relative power over their work conditions and access to the materials and training to control their job would establish caseworkers as professionals. Faith pointed to how perceptions of care linked to resources and physical environments. According to Faith, SIL apartment conditions affected not only staff perceptions but also how clients felt about themselves. Other workers echoed this sentiment on many occasions. They believed that top-level officials communicated lack of care and concern for clients when they forced families to live in dangerous and pest-infested surroundings. Faith asked, "Have they even seen what these girls' apartments look like?" Case managers and clients were largely unaware of the structural challenges that prevented SIL administrators from renting in higher-income environments.

Another SIL worker suggested that the program should show the girls better environments; it should rent a van and take the moms on trips to the art museum and other cultural venues. After lively discussion among the staff, Faith expressed her enthusiasm about the enrichment activities but said when she returned to her office she would feel discouraged again. I observed other fleeting moments when staff members explored possibilities for meaningful interactions with clients. Staff members rarely implemented these ideas because of limited funding, staff shortages, and liability concerns. For instance, the agency could not legally transport babies and was unable to pay for and coordinate babysitters. These circumstances prevented participation in cultural events and other fun excursions. Caseworkers constantly put out fires (figuratively on most occasions but, on one occasion, literally), as program crises took precedence. We will explore the implications of program crises in greater detail in chapter 2.

Dangerous, underresourced, and demoralized environments hindered case management, as did cumbersome communication practices. In the narrative opening this chapter, Helen complained that workers had to repeat tasks because of administrative errors and complicated procedural pathways. Staff implemented agency services and submitted reports through multistep pathways across different program settings and SIL staff hierarchy. It was common for information or paperwork to get confused or lost. As Helen indicated, this convoluted process to securing necessary resources for one's job often led to delays. For example, in order to purchase the key she would need to enter the apartment building, she had submitted a check request. Purportedly, her program manager had signed this request and the SIL administrative assistant had faxed it to the agency's business office. The financial department at the business office was in charge of issuing the check. Yet several weeks later, Helen had not received it, leaving her without direct access to the apartment building from which she worked.

Given the high staff turnover rates, both program managers and caseworkers were often newly hired and tended to be confused about their roles and responsibilities. New program managers were unclear about program policies and procedures, as Teresa noted in the vignette above. Teresa viewed her staff as unwilling to work, a common perception across participants in administrative positions. Supervisors expressed their feelings of being overwhelmed and overworked. In our conversations, they did not show that they recognized the ways their staff may have experienced similar challenges.

The relative lack of long-standing SIL employees at all levels meant that few possessed rich institutional and "case specific" knowledge. Caseworkers' and supervisors' perception of themselves as overworked and undertrained fueled a cyclical process in which the cadre of SIL workers at any given time were incapable of preparing new hires. One case manager, Candice, was a recent hire at the time we talked and ended up staying in her position only a couple of months. Candice was African American, just out of college, and in her mid-twenties. She had had a baby when she was a teenager and had lived in the foster care system. As a youth, she had been in an independent living program. She confided to me that she was unsure how to complete the children's Individual Service Plans. Candice needed to assess the children's development and determine whether they had reached certain milestones. She had limited knowledge about child development, and her supervisor had not taught her how to recognize "age appropriate" behavior.

A couple of days after we talked about child ISPs, I overheard Candice in a conversation with a more experienced SIL caseworker while we waited for a staff training session to begin on "safety in the field." CYS required caseworkers to complete an inventory form on every SIL apartment, each week. The forms were stored in each client's case file in the staff offices. CYS had abruptly changed the form, and the new form included a more detailed inventory checklist to evaluate the physical condition of each SIL apartment. The program managers expected their caseworkers to condense several months of apartment notes into these new forms. Candice exclaimed in frustration that she had stayed up most of the previous night converting all her old notes. She worried because the new form required information that she had not noted originally. The other caseworker responded that she had simply made up the unknown information.

Caseworkers who remained on the job learned that staying up all night completing paperwork was unsustainable. Given the expectations and demands of the job, many of these caseworkers learned to cut corners and manage an impression of compliance. These impressions were not always accurate. Yet caseworkers coped in a fear-driven climate. Procedures changed repeatedly, and high stakes were attached to official expectations for compliance. At the same time, these expectations tended to be unrealistic given the constraints faced on the ground. I am not justifying false documentation, but I want to show the real barriers and constraints that caseworkers faced and the contexts within which they made their everyday decisions.

SIL Staff Meeting: Dilemmas of Responsibility

Repeatedly, administrators asked caseworkers to accommodate to shifting documentation requirements and policies, even though the program did not give workers adequate training in how to complete these tasks. Vignettes from a staff meeting illuminate how tensions arose from insufficient staff training, lack of institutional history, and unclear guidelines for case management. The meeting also shows something less tangible: the social and psychological distance between program managers and their caseworkers. Jane, a middle-aged African American program manager, led a Monday staff meeting at the SIL administrative office. The agency had hired Jane only a few months earlier to accompany Teresa as joint program manager. Before joining the agency, Jane had worked with boys in the local juvenile justice system for many years. Teresa was not present at this meeting. The seating arrangement in the room indicated the social divide. Jane sat alone on one side of a long conference table, and seven staff members and I sat clustered and crowded together on the other side of the table. Nobody sat next to Jane. Just before the meeting began, Jane asked one of the caseworkers to move to her side of the table so she could close the sliding doors to the room. The worker pulled her chair in to the crowded side and closed the door but did not move to the open space next to Jane.

Jane began the meeting by handing out paper copies of the SIL program standards of care, one for each apartment site. As she distributed these, she said she expected the workers to pass city and state inspections because they would have access to the standards. The staff members gazed at Jane with blank, deadpan stares. Jane asked if anyone had any questions and nobody responded. She explained another shift in CYS policy around admission of new clients to SIL. CYS would keep the waiting list for the program, prioritizing the order in which the SIL program would admit clients. This was a change from the prior policy in which the agency maintained control over the long waiting list. Jane explained a few other changes, which involved CYS's gaining authority over program decisions. Although Jane did not articulate this, these new procedures would not only reduce the case managers' workload but also limit their power. Jane finished by asking the staff how this sounded to them. She received no reply. Finally, she asked whether staff believed the changes would be beneficial. Again, everyone in the room was silent. I noted my own discomfort during these awkward silences. On prior occasions, several caseworkers mentioned to me that they disliked Jane. They believed that she always favored the clients and did not consider caseworker needs or perspectives on their clients. When staff did not feel valued as professionals, they tended to begrudge their supervisors' attention to their clients. In a demoralized setting, social actors (including both clients and SIL staff at different levels) competed for respect and dignity. The politics of care involved a vying for concern from higher-ups across SIL environments.

At this point, Jane changed the subject and opened up discussion around "site-specific issues." The tone in the room shifted dramatically. Many attendees became animated and talkative as the discussion quickly jumped from one issue to another. While caseworkers had an opportunity to vent and identify problems experienced on the job, I noted an absence of actual problem solving. Several caseworkers attempted to clarify their responsibilities around distribution of such varied items as condoms, food, milk, clothing vouchers, heat, keys, high chairs, and Women, Infants, and Children (WIC) supplements. Caseworkers were unsure when clients should receive clothing vouchers, how many they should receive, and how the SIL caseworkers should acquire these vouchers from the CYS agency. The most experienced caseworker responded that some CYS caseworkers were forthcoming with clothing vouchers and others were stingy, again pointing to an inequitable gap in policy implementation. Caseworkers complained that the building landlords were cheap and did not heat their buildings. The girls used their ovens to heat the apartments, which presented safety hazards. Helen said she had submitted three check requests for front door keys to the Evergreen building. She had not received the needed check after four months of attempts. She emphasized that nine clients needed keys. Many of these mothers had newborns. "This just isn't fair," she said matter-of-factly.

Throughout the discussion, Jane repeatedly marked down problems. She responded to the caseworkers' uncertainty about procedures by acknowledging her own lack of knowledge and training. She said a central program manual was needed to explain all required services. However, she did not confront a key obstacle to creating an accurate, centralized manual: as evidenced at this particular meeting, policies, procedures, and paperwork in the SIL program constantly changed to meet the shifting requirements of the program's public regulator, CYS. The lack of institutional history among the SIL program's mostly new hires created barriers to comprehensive programming and an inability to understand what the job entailed.

A heated discussion ensued about program resources and services. This illuminated a debate that surfaced repeatedly during my fieldwork. I also recall this dilemma from my tenure as program manager. Staff held diverse views on how to achieve the SIL program's goals. Program documents and rhetoric emphasized individual responsibility, which I will discuss in more detail in chapter 3. At the same time, staff members had different ideas about how to promote independence. Many caseworkers believed that the program perpetuated the young mothers' dependency on the system by giving "free handouts." Everyone seemed to agree that certain resources, such as heat and building keys, were required. There was disagreement around other provisions. For instance, the mothers received weekly stipend checks from the SIL program, which they were expected to use to buy food and milk. The program staff was legally mandated to provide these basic necessities, even if the mothers spent their checks on other things. Some staff felt that they did a disservice to their clients through "hand-holding." They questioned what the adolescents learned when staff did not allow them to face the natural consequences of bad decision making. Some workers indicated that once the mothers left the program, they would not know how to budget appropriately, would not understand appropriate consequences, and would be unprepared to live independently. These workers perceived hypocrisy in the program's mission and in their roles as state agents.

However, even among caseworkers, there was no consensus. Workers debated and disagreed about resource provisions. For instance, during the staff meeting, Faith reminded her coworkers that all the clients were eligible for and should receive WIC, adding that this would alleviate some of the food and milk shortages. She was unable to fathom why some of the girls were not taking advantage of WIC supplements. Rebecca responded that several of the moms were too embarrassed to visit the WIC office. Faith suggested that the SIL program arrange for WIC to deliver provisions directly to the apartment sites. Rachelle exclaimed forcefully that there were numerous WIC offices across many city neighborhoods. She implied that the mothers should take personal responsibility for picking up their own WIC supplies. Faith had the last word as she interjected that the kids didn't need to suffer just because the moms were "trifling."

Generally, in such debates, administrative supervisors tended to emphasize the legal constraints faced by the program and the necessity to manage risk appropriately. They would underscore that workers must provide all basic necessities despite their personal beliefs and should document these provisions in writing. The supervisors focused on the program's role as a state agent and its legal responsibility to guarantee that clients had access to food and milk at all times.

Multiple Regulators, Mixed-Up Implications

Case managers' bodily and verbal resistance to Jane was informed by their sense of powerlessness to execute interventions. They did not feel their supervisor supported them. Also, caseworkers believed that program managers protected mothers from experiencing natural consequences of their bad decisions (e.g., of spending stipend checks "irresponsibly" or not picking up WIC food). Many case managers asserted that the program disserved youth because it did not show them how to survive in the real world. Program managers felt their hands were tied by liability pressures.

As Helen reported, the presence of drugs in an apartment did not consistently result in a client's discharge. Despite a program manual that dictated systematic procedures for addressing noncompliance, workers complained that program managers either ignored or excused clients who broke the rules. Teresa, the program manager, found drugs in Tomeka's SIL apartment. Considerable confusion followed. Tomeka, an eighteen-year-old African American mother of a four-month-old son at the time of this incident, had just learned she was pregnant again. By the time I spoke to Rebecca, Tomeka's case manager, she informed me that Tomeka would be discharged from the SIL program in two days. I visited Tomeka in her apartment and asked whether she would like me to accompany her to court to advocate for her next placement. She accepted my offer, declaring that she didn't know why she was going to be "kicked out." I said that it seemed to be because of the drugs. Tomeka countered in a defensive tone, saying that the drugs belonged to her boyfriend and that she had not known they were in her apartment. Tomeka was clearly distraught, particularly because different SIL workers had spoken of different consequences. According to Tomeka, when Teresa found the drugs, she did not mention discharge. Nel informed Tomeka that she would be put on a thirty-day contract, during which she would need to demonstrate improved behavior. Later the same day, Rebecca told her to start packing because she was going to be discharged.

I was ill the day Tomeka appeared in court, and I could not accompany her. That same afternoon, Rebecca called me and expressed her embarrassment and frustration. According to Rebecca, the judge had admonished her for trying to get Tomeka discharged. Unbeknownst to Rebecca, Tomeka's probation officer had spoken to Teresa, the SIL program manager. Together, the PO and Teresa decided to retain Tomeka in the program, but they failed to communicate this decision to Rebecca. Rebecca explained that this decision was inconsistent with what the PO had previously told her, namely, that Tomeka would be discharged and her baby would be taken under the custody of CYS. Rebecca believed that she was made to look like the "bad guy" when she had simply followed discharge orders from her supervisors.

This experience illuminates the confusion and miscommunication that resulted from the multiple levels of regulators. Across levels within both the private agency and the juvenile justice system, workers engaged in decision-making processes. As caseworkers and supervisors articulated different consequences for the drugs' presence in her apartment, Tomeka felt vulnerable and uncertain of her fate in the program. She wondered whether she would even maintain custody of her child. Given multiple regulators and uncertain consequences for breaking rules, participants felt confused about their roles and responsibilities.

Multiple Chances: Comprehensive Problem Solving

On several occasions, supervisors fielded caseworkers' concerns about lenient responses to clients' "bad" behavior. During one such encounter, the SIL director, Beth Spellman, attempted to contextualize the administrators' efforts to retain clients, even after clients broke rules. She explained that the agency had always worked with the most vulnerable populations. Beth was the only staff member in a supervisory position who had worked for the agency for many years. Officially, she was not responsible for leading SIL staff meetings. She did so on occasion when program managers were unavailable. Beth communicated the agency's philosophy, stating that it was "no secret" that Visions offered girls multiple chances. Beth, who was in her late fifties, had been a social service provider for much of her adult life. Her youthful and energetic attitude made her appear many years younger. She repeatedly confided in me, bemoaning administration and saying she missed interacting directly with young families. Beth had worked her way up from her white working-class background to become one of the top-ranking directors at Visions. She remained strongly committed to serving clients, even as her rank in the agency mostly eliminated everyday interactions with young families.

Beth felt that imposing appropriate consequences required responding to each case individually and flexibly. Clients needed to be given multiple chances to learn from their mistakes and failures. One could not alleviate in a short time the effects of trauma caused over a long period. Beth depicted this disparity by holding her hands very close together and then moving them as far apart as she could manage as her voice became louder. The program was publicly mandated to facilitate positive youth outcomes, and she suggested that youth could reach these only with consistent support from staff. She lamented that clients aged out of SIL without diplomas or housing. The program could not justify these poor outcomes. Several caseworkers nodded in agreement, clearly amenable to Beth's suggestions. The caseworkers' visible receptiveness to Beth contrasted starkly with their closed response to Jane. Beth was able to contextualize the program's approach because of her deep organizational knowledge, while Jane's newness at the agency limited her ability to explain programmatic decisions.

Brian Littlechild argues that comprehensive risk management can be successful in service climates only where there is openness to grappling with difficult and complex human issues. Caseworkers must be able to address their fears openly with administrators in a culture of support rather than blame (Littlechild 2008). Beth created this type of environment as she emphasized collective, flexible, individually responsive problem solving. She explained the reasons behind giving multiple chances to clients. On other occasions, she mentioned the need to keep the program at full capacity. CYS paid the SIL program a per diem rate for each enrolled client. Multiple discharges would increase funding deficits for the program, as CYS did not pay SIL for empty apartments. Retaining clients was an economic necessity, even when they broke the rules.

Beth was a great resource, but leading SIL staff meetings was not a role she could play consistently, as it was the responsibility of the program managers. Beth did not address the programmatic barriers to case-specific problem solving. Given the staff shortages, insufficient training, and lack of institutional and case-specific knowledge among staff, the approach Beth described was largely infeasible.

The Social Context of Care

Margaret Beale Spencer and colleagues (2006) suggest that feeling competent is a basic human need. Workers doubted their authenticity as professionals, as they were insufficiently trained, lacked necessary resources, and did not receive consistent administrative guidance or support. Their workspaces compromised their perceptions of autonomy and self-respect. Confusing organizational structures and bureaucratic hierarchies hindered their motivations and ability to provide effective services.

Young clients did not generally perceive the structural barriers affecting their case managers, as case managers did not always understand the legalistic and system-level constraints experienced by their supervisors. Further, staff members did not communicate their feelings of powerlessness to their clients. Clients tended to believe that their workers simply did not care about them. One young mother described the program to me as a "joke," because staff members did not uphold program rules and she did not feel protected by SIL staff. She experienced her living environment as chaotic and threatening.

Michael Herzfeld (2005) points to the wide range of objectives and self-interests that individual officials pursue. Just as clients make decisions and act on the basis of various motives, so do administrators and caseworkers. It is impossible to determine whether a "class" (373) of individuals (administrators, caseworkers, or clients) acts on the basis of morally just intentions or deceitful, self-interested ones. Individuals express a range of motives, which change over time and contexts. Rather, we must consider the consequences of systematic inequalities on the standpoints of youth and their workers, regardless of any particular participant's good or bad intentions.

Bureaucratic procedures, SIL program inequalities, and environmental and legalistic threats influenced the process of caring for others. Physical, social, and representational aspects of context shaped a participant's ability to care, as well as a recipient's ability to perceive being cared for. Clients, caseworkers, and administrators shared their perceptions of which workers cared or did not care about young families in SIL. During an interview, Jasmine, a client, named the SIL staff members who cared about her and other clients. She mentioned Helen. Although she did not give the names of staff members she perceived to be uncaring, she described them. Jasmine included herself as part of a group of young mothers as she said the following:

> Some of these case managers and all that, they . . . I don't feel as though they should work here because they don't understand what we are going through. Like all right, say they are all up in our face, up in my face [saying], "I finished school. I didn't have no kids. I didn't get pregnant when I was young." [In response, Jasmine said,] "All right, that is you. We kids make mistakes."

Jasmine marked uncaring caseworkers as those who judged and stigmatized a youth's behaviors and decisions. These workers identified themselves as better than their clients, and Jasmine was critical of the ways these workers "Othered" her and fellow clients.

Janile, an African American SIL staff member, worked at the smallest SIL apartment site. She told me she loved the girls as if they were her own children. Janile explained her self-proclaimed "tough love" approach. Several of her clients, who perceived her as a grandmotherly figure, shared their appreciation for Janile. They claimed that Janile would "stay on them" to do well in the program. Janile went above and beyond her part-time, live-in staff duties and taught "her girls" how to keep their apartments clean and how to cook.[6] She also spent countless hours visiting with her residents and offering advice.

SIL participants expressed care in many ways. Yet they could not sustain these acts evenly throughout the program because of inconsistent policies, miscommunication, stigma discourses, and material deficits. I observed "caring" qualities shift across contexts and change over time even when expressed by the same particular individuals. For example, Jasmine and several other youth identified Helen as a "caring" staff person, even though I witnessed Helen speak disparagingly about particular girls. She appeared to gossip about the sexual and drug-related behaviors of particular youth, only in the company of other adult staff members. Helen's comments seemed to draw on and reinforce stigmas about adolescent mothers and poor youth of color, the same stigmas that Jasmine bemoaned when they were expressed by uncaring staff. I never observed Helen directly disrespect a client. In fact, I observed the opposite—she would sit for hours listening to and comforting a youth. She would assist moms in a number of other ways, delivering diapers and taking clients shopping for food and clothes. Helen felt overburdened by the many obligations of her job, and it is important to understand how the context in which she worked shaped the moments when she would complain or gossip. These occurrences coexisted with her many generous and kind acts.

Conclusion

This chapter has explored how structural and environmental obstacles faced on the job were components of SIL administration, case management, and care among participants. A general inability to sustain long-lasting and meaningful relationships also hindered care. Identifying "caring" caseworkers and getting rid of the "uncaring" ones would not improve service provision overall. As I noted above, care was contingent on context. Despite variations in compassion and commitment among individuals, "audit cultures" (Herzfeld 2005) and a "culture of fear" compromised a general ethos of care in the SIL program (Littlechild 2008). SIL environments shaped interactions in ways that compromised concern, irrespective of any individual worker's intentions. I do not wish to excuse the egregious behaviors of some staff members. Caseworkers who abuse clients should always face severe consequences. Care should be an essential aspect of any relationship between an official and a client or a supervisor and a caseworker. Rather, I suggest that an individualized approach to care will not address the effects of structural inequalities and stigma narratives. Fragmentation within and between bureaucracies compromised the kind acts of participants and limited effective service provision. I turn next to further consideration of spatial fragmentation and how youth coped along with their case managers in underresourced, dangerous SIL program settings.

The Better Places Don't Want Teen Moms

Invisible Lives, Hidden Program Spaces

The SIL program rented apartments in low-income, racially segregated areas, where there was a significant drug trade. In an interview, Beth Spellman, the SIL director, talked about the difficulties of leasing apartments for the SIL program:

> That's always an issue because, with the per diem rates that we get [from CYS], we can only afford to pay like X number of dollars for rent, and that really limits the quality of housing that we can do. . . . So we wind up being in places where there tend to be roach problems and drug problems, and I don't know, unless we eventually get our own building, you know that we'll be able to get away from that stuff. And you know the other issue, even if we could afford something better, the better places don't want teen moms. . . . They really do look at the girls as failures and potential trouble, and they know that the girls are coming from troubled backgrounds. It's not always money; sometimes it's just basically, "No we don't want you here, not in our backyard. Yeah, we feel sorry for these young girls, and we hope somebody takes you, but we're not going to."

The administrator spoke about the limiting social, cultural, and economic factors that mediated the type of apartments available for the SIL program. In other words, lack of funds from the city's child welfare agency was one factor that limited the program's rentals. Racist and classist perceptions among the public also hindered the program's location. Many private leasing agencies were unwilling to rent to a program for teenage mothers and their children. These stigma-based perceptions have historical roots in the residential and rental housing markets. For decades, leasing agencies have steered low-income minority populations into segregated areas of cities. Over time, prejudice has upheld residential segregation and discrimination based on race and class (Dreier, Mollenkopf, and Swanstrom 2004). These larger obstacles contributed to an environment in which many SIL participants did not feel safe.

Informal Residents and Social Networks

It was common for boyfriends (or girlfriends and family members) to reside in SIL apartments with mothers and children, even though this violated SIL program rules. Caseworkers repeatedly struggled to enforce occupancy rules. In one case, an entire extended family lived in a one-bedroom apartment. The client's mother, mother's boyfriend, and sibling resided along with the client, her boyfriend, and the client's two children in the SIL apartment. In many other instances, friends or romantic partners would take up temporary residency with clients. Across SIL sites, live-in boyfriends were particularly common. Widespread cohabitation with unofficial residents occurred, in part, because of an affordable-housing crisis in the city. Furthermore, case managers could not logistically exercise extensive oversight because of the structure of SIL residences. Single-occupancy apartments in privately managed community buildings created a compartmentalized and open residential structure.

SIL workers often bemoaned the presence of these "outsiders," noting the violence, guns, and drugs they tended to bring with them. Even though caseworkers were frustrated by the "problems" outsiders caused, many accepted the presence of unofficial residents and tried to help them achieve better lives. Irrespective of the workers' shifting perceptions, caseworkers remained powerless to enforce the removal of outsiders from program residences. Although administrators were at least superficially aware of unofficial residents, spatial separation allowed administrators to ignore this breach of program policy. As we saw in chapter 1, administrators worked from a separate SIL office in a suburban location.

In SIL, because a wide gap separated official record keeping and performance requirements from the resources to meet these goals, moms and their case managers constructed their own informal social networks. Further, official rules did not always respond or connect to the realities of young families living in the SIL program. For example, Rachelle, a case manager at the Chatham SIL apartment site, described the ways she modified SIL program policy to account for the constant presence of men in the apartments.

RACHELLE: So we have drug dealers in our building. It has gotten better as I build a relationship with the girls. You know [I tell the girls to] try to stay away from them [drug dealers]. If you have a male companion that is selling drugs, tell him not to do it here. Tell him to go somewhere else. And like I was telling Beth [the SIL program director] the other day, you know what, you holler holler holler, you tell the girls, "He cannot be here, he cannot be here," and in actuality, he doesn't have a place to go. . . . You can go into an apartment five times in one day and tell him to leave, but who is to say he's going to leave. He might walk down the hall and go into another apartment. And when you don't have someone over the top of you coming out there to visit, coming out there to say, "Well, you have to leave and there's no if ands buts about it. If you are caught in this building again, we will call the cops and have you arrested for trespassing." That has never happened since I have been here. So instead of just keep saying, "Leave leave leave leave," [she says to the guys,] "You might as well stay and help clean up." It's not helping them much; the "leave leave leave leave" doesn't do any good because they're not leaving. So, you're like, let him stay, and just say, "Well, these are the rules for you too," and you become case manager to the guys.

LAUREN: So is that what you have found to happen?

RACHELLE: Oh, yeah, I have to tell them, "You do this, this, and this, hopefully, you'll get a job. Can you come up here and sign for this and take the medical cards back upstairs and tell [the mother that] Ms. Rachelle sent them? Tell her to call me later on if she has any questions. Why were you fighting last night? You know better with children in the hallway."

I mean, you're a case manager to them too, so if you have twenty-three people and you add on their boyfriends, that's more.

LAUREN: And their children, so you probably have about . . . I don't know.

RACHELLE: Whatever, there are so many. [She laughs]. It's too much. I mean they respect me now since we've grown. But then you have outsiders that come in that don't respect you. They don't care who you are.

LAUREN: Outsiders, meaning?

RACHELLE: Guy outsiders. They are trying to feel their way in or see who they can hook up with. And you'll be like, "No, that's not happening here. You need to leave." And they'll be like, "And you are?" And I say, "And you are?"

LAUREN: When you said that you established respect.

RACHELLE: Not so much respect, I have established a good relationship. I support them to encourage them to move forward. It takes time to get to know each one individually. Just to show them that if you go to school today, I will call them later in the evening and ask, "How was school? Did you have fun? Really, tell me all about it."

Rachelle offered a number of justifications for breaking the official rule that prohibited male cohabitants. She felt empathy for the young men and understood that well-being was interconnected between the children, mothers, and the mothers' male companions. The stated program policy limited workers' caseload to a maximum of ten clients (and their children). However, because of high worker turnover and problems retaining caseworkers, Rachelle's caseload far exceeded this limit. She found it infeasible to enforce the rule prohibiting the men, because administrators did not back her up. Even administrators did not have the authority to force men out of a building the agency did not own. Rachelle spoke about developing a rapport with these men so she could establish her role as an authority figure and mentor. Such authority and guidance helped her maintain relative order and cohesion at her site. Her narrative complicated the stereotype of the predatory young black male, and she conveyed an understanding that both young women and men struggled with repercussions of poverty, racism, and abuse.

Rachelle's practice was not unusual among caseworkers at the three SIL apartment sites. At Evergreen, caseworkers adjusted their practices to use unofficial residents for assistance. On several occasions, I observed young men enter the office alone. The men would retrieve from caseworkers documents such as health-care cards or other information for the moms or children. Caseworkers developed supportive relationships with some of these informal residents, who were consistently involved in the day-to-day life of the program. For example, when one young mother died during childbirth, her infant's father remained in contact with Helen, one of the SIL workers. His connection with Helen had begun when he was an unofficial resident, living with his girlfriend in a SIL apartment. In fact, before the tragedy, Helen and I had visited with the soon-to-be father when he came to the office to retrieve the client's weekly stipend check. We listened as he articulated his concerns and hopes for the future. We offered advice on how he could get his high school diploma and begin a career as a chef. Helen continued (unofficially) to provide a listening ear and emotional support to this young man, even after the client passed away. He took on the task of parenting his infant son alone.[1]

Interestingly, Rachelle, Helen, and other caseworkers in SIL were not alone in breaking the rules when the rules were not working. Caseworkers and clients believed that SIL program rules were impractical and sometimes unfair given the realities they faced on the ground. Lisa Dodson (2009) conducted interviews with hundreds of working poor people, as well as with the business managers, health-care providers, and teachers who supervised or interacted with working-poor adults, their children, or both. Dodson found a common "moral underground" (5) across these distinct public and private sectors. The moral underground includes the tactics developed by workers and managers to offer greater justice to working-poor families. She frames these strategies as everyday resistances, particularly as official rules are frequently broken. In the moral underground, human benefits are placed above maximum financial gains and the rationing of care. Individual and community moral codes informed these underground tactics. The interviewed workers acknowledged that justice often runs counter to official rules, which disadvantage families already burdened by poverty. I too found a moral underground at play in the SIL program. Yet my participants' narratives complicated the nature of hidden tactics. Sometimes, strategies stemmed from a commitment to justice, while in other instances, hidden actions stemmed from injustice. I explore the underside of an underground later in the chapter.

Rachelle and other caseworkers believed that good relationships with official and unofficial residents helped them guide their SIL communities. Given the reality of fluid apartment and community boundaries, caseworkers broadened the scope of their roles and their definition of SIL community. As we explored during her interview, Rachelle built fruitful relationships through communicating care in a number of ways. She contrasted these interactions with the lack of respect she received from male outsiders.

Rachelle complicated the duality of insider and outsider roles as she located some cooperating males as informal residents and other unfamiliar males as outsiders. She described these outsider men as a constant source of threat. Rachelle did not have authority over outsiders, who might challenge the delicate balance she sought to achieve at her SIL apartment site. To maintain stability, she had to repeatedly negotiate relationships with outsider males as they became more involved with the young families and gradually began to take on roles as informal residents. SIL caseworkers' emotional response to the young men oscillated from sympathy to indignation, reflecting the workers' diverse interactions with them.

Familiar Zones and Formal Zones

Participants hid rule-breaking behaviors and violence, as well as a "moral underground" (Dodson 2009: 5) in the familiar zones at the apartment sites. In order to meet personal needs and create the impression of compliance, participants used what Michael Herzfeld (2005: 372) calls a "zone of familiar ease" and what I term a familiar zone. Herzfeld characterizes a "zone of familiar ease" as a space where "bureaucrats" use their personal agency to "patch up, muddle through, and simply cope" with the rigidity of state demands. Herzfeld explores the roles of bureaucrats, but I examine the ways clients, case managers, and program managers together used program familiar zones. Familiar zones, constructed contexts of "bearable life" (Herzfeld 2005: 372), arose in relatively unregulated settings, like the program's residential sites and the program's GED class.

Social distance created familiar zones in the SIL program. As we saw in chapter 1, social distance was caused by two primary conditions: spatial divisions within the SIL program and hierarchical relations of power. Many top-level administrators and officials rarely (if ever) visited the residential sites where young families lived. Hierarchy within the organization created social distance through the inequalities between programming sites and administrative sites. Three conditions shaped the necessity for participants to hide decision making and rule breaking in familiar zones: a culture of fear and blame; high stakes attached to meeting official goals; and a gap that separated official goals from the social, economic, and organizational resources to meet goals.

When an inspector visited an apartment to conduct an audit, these spaces would momentarily lose their qualities as familiar zones. The power dynamic would shift as a result of the presence of an authority figure. In other words, familiar zones existed along a spatial and social continuum that shifted over time. Authority too existed on a continuum, with auditors having more power than program managers and case managers. James Scott (1998) explains how government administrators construct a formal zone, which exists at the opposite end of the spectrum from familiar zones. Officials create formal zones through techniques that include procedural protocols, paperwork, record keeping, outcome measures, and audits. Such tactics regulate social reality as they reduce, assimilate, and transform it into legible official forms. Scott contends that bureaucrats maintain power through administrative processes. Administrative acts produce a formal, objective reality that necessarily ignores contradictory, messy aspects of social life.

Young mothers, often along with their caseworkers, learned how to negotiate formal and familiar zones by reconstituting policies on the ground. In familiar zones, they hid from officials the violence they experienced, the informal social networks they necessarily relied on, and the compromised school conditions they faced. They did this not because they agreed with the state of their conditions but to sustain an *impression* of compliance. Mothers risked becoming homeless and losing custody of their children.

Implications of Familiar Zones

The widespread presence of unofficial residents in apartments indicated the lack of comprehensive support from the SIL program and child welfare system. It also pointed to something less tangible: the inflexibility of program ideals in contrast to clients' actual experiences of daily life and family. The SIL model was based on one conceptualization of the family unit: a single adolescent mother and her child or children. Actual family units included young men, fathers, and friends and extended family members (and these configurations changed over time). The SIL family model was based on stereotypes about the unsuitability of poor young men of color. The state did not consider these men deserving of assistance and implemented a policy that excluded them from sharing in services provided to the mothers and children. Thus, clients would hide from scrutiny these young men and all other informal residents.

Clients depended on their unofficial residents for several types of support, including childcare, companionship, and economic resources. Almost every young woman I spoke with asserted that the sixty-two-dollar stipend she received from the program per week (for one mom and child) was insufficient. Many young mothers were afraid to be alone with their children, and they felt particularly unsafe in the apartment buildings where they resided. One youth kept a large knife above her doorframe. When asked about it, she explained she needed it to protect her kids in case the apartment was invaded. Clients desired the companionship and protection they found with their unofficial residents. Yet, paradoxically, some of these same men would batter them. When I noted this tension to one young mom she responded that at least her boyfriend wouldn't let anyone else hurt her. Over time, I became increasingly aware of numerous incidents of domestic violence, visible in kicked-in doors and ransacked apartments.

The girls had complicated relationships with their men, which they described in terms of love, reliance, and abuse. They desired companionship but also felt trapped. One young mother told me that she loved her boyfriend and understood that he was "a product of his environment." She claimed that she would be joined with him for life because she was having his baby and he threatened to kill her if she ever left him. She believed that he would. Another young mother compelled her boyfriend to tattoo her name on his body. She explained the marking would tie them together and deter him from cheating on her in the future. One youth felt that she could not resist or get away from the man who abused her. He was also the father of her child. This man forced her to stay inside the SIL apartment and did not let her work or attend school. His control directly opposed the SIL program's requirements (and her personal goals) to attend high school and work at a part-time job. Again, she was caught. She shared with me her relief when her child's father was locked up. Once he was behind bars, she got a job and reenrolled in school. He was released shortly afterward and the cycle continued.

Participants' perceptions of safety were constantly in flux, in part because of the presence of unofficial residents. Jasmine, a SIL mother, shared an experience that speaks to what happens when staff authority breaks down in a familiar zone, as was often the case. Because workers were unable to protect clients, this reality sustained a culture of fear among participants.

Jasmine lived at Evergreen with her daughter, a toddler. Jasmine reported that after a quarrel with another SIL resident, Khadisha, Khadisha's live-in boyfriend pulled out a gun to threaten Jasmine. Jasmine grumbled about the boyfriend's living in a SIL apartment, complaining that he was not even supposed to be in the program. But he was threatening her life. Jasmine's complaint seemed well founded. On many occasions, I tutored Khadisha in her apartment and had witnessed the boyfriend coming or going. His clothing and shoes were spread across the apartment. Jasmine recounted the incident to the SIL live-in staff member, who reportedly exclaimed, "Well, how I know if he got a gun or not?" She did not address the issue further. Jasmine indicated that she reported the threat to Jane, one of the SIL program managers, and to her PO. The officials agreed to hold a meeting to discuss the incident. Jasmine did not know whether this meeting would take place, as some time had passed and she had received no news. She said Khadisha's boyfriend threatened her a second time:

> Because the first time he did it, he was like, "Who the F said I put my hands on my girlfriend, who the F . . . [Jasmine actually says "F"] He pulled the gun out on us and we ran. So the second time, my daughter was in here [the apartment], and I walked Shakiya [another mother in the SIL program] to the elevator and I left my door open. What if my daughter would have ran out here when he pulled the gun on us? And Shakiya was like, "Come on, let's go tell the live-in." All right, the first time I told the live-in she didn't do nothing, so why should we tell her again?

When young mothers, such as Jasmine, communicated their concerns and SIL workers did not address them, the workers sent the message that their clients' concerns were unimportant or invalid. The live-in may have felt powerless to address the situation. In fact, several case managers repeatedly bemoaned their lack of power and their fear of the clients' male companions. They attributed this fear to the wide availability of guns, but staff did not openly communicate these feelings to their clients. Staff tended to keep their experiences of vulnerability hidden to maintain a semblance of authority over the program. The lack of expedient follow-through by the administrator and PO perpetuated Jasmine's perception that the program staff would not protect her or her child. Jasmine's comments were illustrative of other complaints I heard from clients. On multiple occasions, mothers grumbled about workers who did not protect them in dangerous situations. Clients tended to take this lack of action personally. As I mentioned in chapter 1, some youth were able to identify individual workers who expressed concern. Even so, they voiced a general sense of being uncared for within the SIL program.

The dangers associated with SIL living environments contributed to a culture of fear. The staff's inability to protect clients contributed to clients' perceptions that they were not safe. Accordingly, familiar zones had two sets of consequences. On the one hand, as in the story told by Rachelle, case managers and mothers coped adaptively, creatively carving out spaces where the youth could live somewhat self-determined lives. They maneuvered skillfully even within organizations that restricted the range of their choices. On the other hand, because these program spaces were hidden, abuse and violence went undetected by authorities.

Because of the high stakes attached to program compliance, daily violence tended to remain within program familiar zones. Here, it was either invisible or ignored by upper-level administrators and public regulators. Although staff inaction sometimes perpetuated violence, in other instances, case managers intentionally inflicted harm on particular mothers. For example, Beth, the SIL program director, told me that a client was denied new mattresses for her children's beds because the case manager in charge did not like the client. Beth discovered this only because she visited the apartment and asked the mom why the bedding was so neglected. The old bedding remained even after Beth told the case manager to order new mattresses.

I learned from clients about other examples in which staff members abused their authority. However, clients did not always report this knowledge to program authorities. They tended to share these accounts with me only after caseworkers left their positions or were fired by the agency. Some youth were afraid they would be discharged for exposing these injustices. Similarly, nondisclosure was common among staff. SIL caseworkers would tell me stories about other staff smoking marijuana with clients or hoarding clients' clothing vouchers for themselves. But they told these stories only after the staff member in question had left the agency. I was perplexed by these silences. When I asked a caseworker about this, she responded casually, suggesting that she did not want to be known as someone who would speak out against another worker.

An ethos of care was compromised by dangerous living conditions and participants' feared retaliation from others (clients and case managers alike). Many did not feel safe enough in their apartments, nor did they feel supported by the program authorities. They therefore did not speak out against injustices they witnessed or experienced in the program. We see the flip side of a moral underground.

Coping in Program Familiar Zones

The SIL program required moms to participate in an educational program, such as high school, GED preparation, vocational education, or college. Program officials put the responsibility for attending school squarely on the clients. However, the youth experienced a key bureaucratic inconsistency: officials expected them to participate in an educational program (and sanctioned them for failing to do so), but the program did not provide all clients with childcare. Upon admission to the SIL program, *dependent* mothers received funding for childcare directly through CYS. *Delinquent* moms, by contrast, followed a rigid protocol and went through several bureaucracies to obtain childcare. First, delinquent youth applied at the office for state-subsidized childcare, which because of their CYS status, was often denied. After processing an application, the office for state-subsidized childcare would send the denial letter to the SIL program. The mom's SIL case manager provided the letter to her SIL supervisor, who then forwarded it to a CYS worker, who might accept the denial. Only then might CYS provide childcare to the young family. Not surprisingly, mothers and case managers found this sequence of tasks nearly impossible to complete successfully.

When SIL did not provide childcare but enforced school completion, mothers took extraordinary measures to attend school while making sure that their children were cared for. Clients used program familiar zones in their attempts. Many moms depended on their unofficial residents for childcare. This reliance filled a gap, as the SIL program and child welfare system neglected childcare for all SIL moms. Some youth arranged care with a shifting network of babysitters, who included boyfriends, girlfriends, other SIL mothers, family members, and even case managers. These babysitters used the SIL apartments to watch the children. The program prohibited babysitters, like other unofficial residents, from occupancy.

Makia, an eighteen-year-old mother of a one-year-old son, provides an illustration of the burdens youth faced when they did not receive childcare resources. She coped using the familiar zone at her apartment site. Soon after entering the SIL program, Makia graduated from high school and was admitted to a university, attendance at which required a one-hour commute each way. At the time of our interview, she had been attending the university for about a month and still did not have daycare. Makia told me the following about her situation:

> I think I've had a lot of help being in this program, and I had a setback by not having any daycare. . . . Now I got to leave my child with different people. Thinking about that while I'm at school, it is hard for me to concentrate. When my teacher gives a lecture, sometimes I find myself wandering and then that leaves me when I get home to have to do extra work because I really wasn't catching on. So I have to re-overlook my notes and . . . I'm here trying to cook for my son, trying to clean up, trying to study. . . . I put him to sleep first, so I can really get some work done, and by the time I lay down it seems like it is time to wake up again. . . . I was having a breakdown about two weeks ago, I was crying because I was just like, I can't do it.

Even though the program supported Makia and her son with an apartment, this same publicly funded care challenged her ability to fully meet educational goals because of the absence of childcare.

When Makia's girlfriend was unable to watch Makia's child in the SIL apartment, her case manager would arrive early to work, at 6:00 A.M., to watch the child. On other days, a SIL program manager paid another SIL mom out of pocket to babysit. One morning, I visited Makia's case manager, Nel, while she watched Makia's son. As I entered the apartment, I instantly noticed the pleasant atmosphere. Makia had arranged the space in a cheerful, child-friendly way, and she had set up a colorful children's tent for her toddler, with several toys inside. With a sigh and a look of exasperation, Nel shared with me their struggle applying for financial aid and said she would do whatever it took to keep Makia in school. She refused to let her fail. Again, we see a moral underground at work in a program familiar zone. After being denied state-subsidized childcare, Makia finally secured daycare from CYS through several SIL staff advocating on her behalf.

An inconsistent mandate that did not provide for her childcare challenged Makia's ability to stay in college. Her social network, which included agency staff going above and beyond their job duties, helped her to remain in school. Her ability to attend college could not be attributed to Makia's personal resilience alone. The extraordinary efforts of several individuals provided the support she needed to offset the absence of government-funded childcare. In fact, the agency recognized Makia publicly for her accomplishments; she received an award at an annual community fund-raising event. Makia was established in the public gaze as an exemplar and positioned to testify to the success of the SIL program.

The agency did not reveal the underside of Makia's story to the public. Soon after the event, I learned that the daycare provision had come too late. Even though Makia was remarkably adept at obtaining assistance from her social network, she had missed too many classes, as babysitters were not always available. She was unable to keep up with her course requirements and withdrew for the fall semester. She told me she planned to reenroll in the spring. Many viewed Makia as a deserving recipient and as a resilient individual. Her caseworkers repeatedly praised her personal motivation, earnestness, and work ethic. Their high regard for her inspired them to act on her behalf. Other youth, whose workers did not hold them in such high esteem, did not receive similar staff assistance. In spite of Makia's personal efficacy, lack of childcare support greatly hindered her college education.

Through Makia's narrative, we see why "success" cannot be attributed to an individual's traits alone but instead should be understood contextually. Resilience is a multidimensional process shaped by individual actions, social policies, and social networks (see, e.g., Debold et al. 1999; Luthar and Cicchetti 2000; Rutter 1993; Spencer et al. 2006; and Ungar 2007). Looking only at the individual ignores the programmatic, systemic, and environmental barriers that shape resiliencies.

Traditional theories of resiliency in many ways perpetuate a myopic focus on the individual. Susan Weseen notes, "The push to discover what makes some children able to swim rather than sink in the turbulent waters of racism and poverty threatens to obscure the dynamics of social and economic injustice" (quoted in Debold et al. 1999: 185). Officials justified the SIL program by the "success" and favored attributes of a few clients, while they ignored institutional inequalities and perpetuated a deficit understanding of most youth in SIL.

Spencer (2006) and Spencer and colleagues (2001, 2003), along with others (e.g., Debold et al. 1999; Luthar and Cicchetti 2000; Rutter 1993; and Ungar 2007), argue that resiliency changes developmentally over time and can be located in the relational contexts in which individual identities emerge. However, little empirical research has documented the ways resiliency takes shape (Olsson et al. 2003; Ungar 2007). If tactics of governance in a SIL program and child welfare system can support or hinder resiliency, then "success" and "failure" must also be understood as socially constructed. If resiliency shifts across contexts, then we need to understand from participants' standpoints which relationships and policies foster well-being. These insights can be used to guide program development to better promote resiliency across nested systems of policies, programs, caseworkers, and youth.

Impression Management

Many participants managed the impressions they created in order to appear compliant with the SIL program. Impression management often came at the expense of actual participation in school. Clients did not uncover the barriers they experienced to engagement because of the high stakes attached to compliance (or at least the appearance of compliance). Several delinquent mothers were unable to obtain childcare support from their informal social networks. Thus, in order to meet the program's educational requirement, they used a different familiar zone: Visions' GED classroom. Tomeka's experience provides one example of how youth were compelled by officials to use this familiar zone. Summoned to court as part of routine judicial oversight, Tomeka, a young delinquent mother, negotiated the schooling requirement with her PO (before entering the courtroom). Tomeka and her PO needed to present a feasible educational plan so that the judge would continue her residential placement in SIL. Tomeka explained that lack of child-care prevented her from attending the classes she needed to complete to earn a high school diploma. Acting as an advocate, I called Jane, a SIL program manager, to ask about educational options for Tomeka. Jane instructed Tomeka to attend Visions' in-house GED classes with her infant until childcare could be obtained. Tomeka was frustrated; she wanted a diploma, not a GED, and she said it would be impossible to concentrate on her schoolwork with her baby in class.

Tomeka's PO aligned with the agency, pushing Tomeka "to meet the agency halfway." Since the agency was working on getting Tomeka daycare, the PO asked her to attend the GED classes and demonstrate her willingness to comply. When Tomeka objected, the PO looked at her sternly and warned that if she wanted an advocate before the judge, then she must promise to attend the program's GED classes. Tomeka quickly muttered her consent. The PO was in a position of relative power to bring Tomeka into agreement and alliance. Only then could they engage together in impression management before the judge. Tomeka affirmed that she was a cooperative and deserving client, even as her progress in school would likely be compromised by her primary responsibility of caring for her baby during class. An empty demonstration of compliance replaced educational participation. Public regulators and the judge would not know the daily experiences of clients attending the program's GED class with their babies.

Tomeka attempted to advocate for herself, but her concerns were dismissed. She lacked the freedom to make educational choices. Most likely, the SIL program manager and PO would have been amenable to Tomeka's preferences if childcare support were available. However, the administrators and Tomeka were enmeshed in a bureaucracy that discriminated against delinquent mothers. This inequality forced delinquent clients, including Makia and Tomeka, to work extra hard at compliance. In spite of individual motivations, informal networks, and impression management, structural barriers compromised educational participation for many delinquent mothers.[2] Because even the most empowered clients struggled, institutional inequities were even more troubling for youth who dealt with personal, medical, or mental health barriers.

Familiar Zones and Regulatory Techniques

Public funds and the SIL program's contract renewal depended on successful audits. Official expectations were often irreconcilable with harsh program realities shaped by funding deficits, organizational obstacles, segregation, and violence. During an audit, government regulators inspected program sites for brief periods and familiar zones would transform temporarily into formal zones.

The legitimacy of the SIL program could be maintained only if contradictory acts that took place in familiar zones remained separate and hidden from public view. SIL participants cooperated in promoting a front of efficiency, not because they agreed with their conditions, but because they experienced pressure to perform in accordance with the front. Mothers feared losing their apartments, even if the apartments were less than adequate. If discharged from the program, they faced heightened risks that included losing custody of their children. During public oversight, SIL program staff and youth cooperated to manage an impression of compliance. One case manager explained how she was able to disguise the presence of unofficial residents from city and state auditors:

> [The case manager tells the mothers,] "An inspector is coming. They are coming to inspect these apartments but make sure they are clean and well taken care of before [the male informal residents] leave, because they can help you." So instead of just throwing [the men] out in the middle of the night, " 'cause I know you don't have nowhere to go, so just leave at nine o'clock [in the morning]. When I pull up, everybody must be out of here. If I have to knock on your door, give you a phone call, did he leave, is everything straight, is everything clean?" And you have to do it like that.

In preparation for inspection, the case manager directed mothers to draw on their male cohabitants for help. Then she enforced the men's brief absence during the audit. The condition of apartments during the scheduled audit constructed the official face of the program.

Within my first couple of months as program manager, I prepared the SIL program for an audit. My supervisor gave me a list of mandated apartment features. Getting the apartments ready involved the quick addition of numerous items, including fire extinguishers, smoke detectors, electric socket protectors, and window screens, among other general improvements. Another case manager discussed her acts of impression management before inspection. She thought the condition of an apartment reflected how a client felt about herself. If a mother was depressed, she might have trouble keeping her apartment up to par. This worker would clean such an apartment for several hours. Before planned inspections, it was common practice for both caseworkers and program managers to assist in apartment facelifts.

The state and CYS both audited the program once a year, during the summer. Auditors were unable to identify treacherous living conditions that persisted over time in program familiar zones. During the winter, clients used their ovens to heat their apartments because landlords underheated facilities to save money. The use of ovens clearly posed safety hazards, but inspectors did not detect such risks during the summer audits. Because auditors were not privy to residential life over time, the audit created the illusion of program legitimacy.

Even auditors socially constructed and negotiated the standards of evaluation. Beth Spellman, the SIL director, described subjectivity in the evaluation process. The city and state were both responsible for determining whether the program adhered to legislated standards. According to Beth, the state enforced standards of residential facility, health and safety, and personnel, as well as mandates pertaining specifically to SIL, special needs populations, and mother-and-baby programming. CYS enforced similar standards, but the city's public agency tended to look more closely at the quality of service provision—evaluating supervision and documentation of service delivery. In order for the SIL program to keep its contract, each year it had to pass both state and CYS inspections. Beth told me the following:

It is interesting, depending upon who the evaluators are, even though they have these written guidelines, there is still a lot of subjectivity. You know, because for instance, we had last year, we had

CYS came out and [they] did their inspection of the physical sites and said it was OK. The state came out about two weeks later and wouldn't license us. So the difference was, CYS, they were people who worked in the inner city, and they know what the realities are in the city. The person who came out from the state came from [a different] county, lived very middle-, maybe upper-middle-class and was totally blown away and couldn't believe that this could be acceptable anywhere. And you know . . . we had to do a lot of work to bring our properties up to her standard and at the same time I think we worked with her, as did her supervisor, to help her bring her standards down to a little more, you're looking at an inner city. . . . Life is really different here. So even though there's written guidelines, there's a lot of subjectivity in how it gets determined.

The purpose of an audit was to enforce *objective* standards of care and facility upkeep and safety. Yet regulatory players did not predetermine standards. Officials negotiated these standards in relation to varied assumptions about what was and was not adequate for whom. Inspectors from the city and state felt differently about adequacy, depending on their familiarity with inner-city or suburban contexts. Beth understood certain conditions as suggesting the "inner city" rather than neglect, racism, and economic inequality. City officials normalized "inner city" conditions and did not classify these environments as discriminatory. Program administrators and evaluators reached compromises regarding conditions of care. The messiness of daily life in the program stayed hidden from regulators, in the program's familiar zones. At the same time, auditors maintained their authority and the program continued to operate.

It was the relative "facade of cohesion" (Scott 1990: 56), rather than any objective reality, that influenced decisions among clients and even workers about "the risks of noncompliance." Young mothers perceived punishment as arbitrary because the program blamed some clients for behaviors that were otherwise routine. This lack of perceived consistency perpetuated a culture of fear in the SIL program. Moms complained about some clients who received special privileges—visitors during nonvisiting hours and the freedom to stay out past curfew. Staff admitted on a few occasions that "the rules could be bent" for motivated youth who were going to school, working, and generally doing well in the program.

I too struggled to understand why SIL staff punished or even discharged some mothers for behaviors regularly engaged in by many others. If the SIL program discharged all clients for rule-breaking behaviors, such as having live-in boyfriends and buying or selling drugs, it would be impossible to keep the program running. As long as noncompliant behaviors remained hidden in familiar zones, the SIL program's administrators turned a blind eye and continued working with the girls. When public officials and private landlords noticed these transgressions, the program would risk losing its contract or leases. This vulnerability required administrators to enforce individual repercussions. Clients could never fully predict the shifting boundary of a familiar zone and which behaviors might become visible. A pervasive culture of fear and blame avoidance shaped risk management procedures in the SIL program.

Tragedy and Uncovering

Early on a Saturday evening, a young man was murdered in the lobby of the Evergreen apartment building, where twenty-five young mothers and their children resided in SIL apartments. The young man who died was a known drug dealer, and several youth reported that he had been killed over a drug-related dispute. A few clients saw the young man's body before it was removed. The live-in staff member was aware of the murder and had documented it in written notes, but she did not contact the case managers or administrators, as the official protocol demanded. Because of the communication breakdown, staff members did not return to the site to assist or comfort program participants until the following Monday. The SIL program director found out about the murder on Sunday evening when she watched the local news. She called the two program managers, who were shocked to learn about the murder. Khadisha, one of the SIL clients, left a phone message for me on Sunday night and told me about the murder when I returned her call on Monday morning.

I quickly made my way to the building. I approached it with apprehension, unsure how I would feel walking into the space where a young man had been killed only days before. In the lobby, to the left side of the entrance, I noticed that a large, colorful shrine had been erected, with burning candles, stuffed animals, and handwritten notes. A couple of people stood silently, looking at the shrine. I joined them for a few moments and then took the elevator to the fourth floor. As I walked into the staff office, I saw that a meeting was already in progress. Teresa and Jane, the two program managers, and all the case managers were gathered. Staff did not allow youth to enter the office. Throughout the meeting, clients continued to knock on the door and were directed to come back later. Subsequently, a couple of youth told me that they did not understand why the staff would not talk to them. It seemed to them as though the staff did not care about them. The program managers explained to the staff their rationale for meeting before they addressed the girls. They wanted the entire staff to be "on the same page" about *how* to talk to the girls in the aftermath of the murder. The young women were not privy to this explanation—they simply felt abandoned.

During the course of this meeting, both program managers emphasized firmly that caseworkers should not tell the clients that the program would be moved to a different site. Neither program manager thought this would be feasible, and they were waiting for correspondence from Beth, the SIL director. One caseworker emphasized that the moms wanted to know how the staff was going to protect them. Teresa, a program manager, responded that the caseworkers should educate the young women about how to be aware of their surroundings. I noticed one caseworker roll her eyes in response. Several staff members emphasized that the girls had been scared for a long time living at Evergreen. They believed the youth would not be satisfied and were going to want a more sufficient response.

Jane, like Teresa, provided her own justification for not moving, beseeching the staff to teach the girls how to live more productively in *these* surroundings. A case manager countered that the girls were influenced by these dangerous surroundings and she asked whether the program could buy its own building or move to a suburban area. Jane dismissed her suggestions as unrealistic. She emphasized that the staff should focus on providing *emotional* support and counseling. According to Jane, youth would need this assistance to cope with their experiences of trauma around the murder. The case managers did not attempt to conceal their frustrations with the program managers' suggestions.

Teresa and Jane were in positions of relative authority in relation to the caseworkers. However, they were not empowered to determine whether the program could be moved from the Evergreen building. Teresa and Jane were SIL program managers and their decision-making capacities were limited by several factors. Because of the staff hierarchy, they would need to get the move approved by the SIL director and the executive director of Visions. Even if they could get the move approved, they would face practical limitations concerning how to quickly move twenty-five families to another rental site. They would need to identify a rental property (or properties) that (1) had enough apartments for all the families, (2) would be willing to rent to a program for teen moms and kids, and (3) would be affordable based on the limited funds provided by CYS. Even if another rental property could be located, the environment would likely be similar to that of the Evergreen building. The chances were slim of finding a willing and affordable private leasing company in a suburban or more affluent urban environment. As noted at the start of this chapter, Beth felt that private rental companies stigmatized the clients and were hesitant to lease to a program for teen moms.

A multifaceted context of limitation framed Teresa's "choice" to advocate adaptation over removing the clients from an inner-city environment. CYS did not provide enough funds to allow the program a wider range of market choices. The situation was further complicated by the racial and class disparities reflected in the Visions agency itself, which was located across urban and suburban sites. Caseworkers did not feel able to protect their clients as long as management continued to house the program in low-income, unsafe, racially segregated urban neighborhoods.

Folk Theories of Change

The program managers and the SIL director, on the one hand, and caseworkers as a group, on the other, expressed diverging views about the relationship of place to client resiliency. These were

connected to the hierarchical positions and corresponding responsibilities of different SIL staff. One's standpoint mattered in one's
construction of knowledge (Sprague 2005). Caseworkers expressed,
before and after the murder, a belief that the program should be
housed in an agency-controlled building or in a better rental location. The caseworkers implied an underlying belief that place mattered. Environments shaped how clients felt about themselves and
how well they functioned as parents, students, and workers. As one
caseworker suggested in an interview,

> We need our own building. . . . I know it's SIL, but it needs to be
> more structured. . . . There needs to be a monitor 24-7, . . . so ev-
> eryone knows what's going on. It would provide a better environ-
> ment for them. They would be much more happy; there would be
> more support. And they would get up to do what they need to do
> to move to self-sufficiency. Because if . . . somebody is constantly
> [monitoring and involved, the girls will feel like,] "OK. They not
> playing. We need to get up and do what we need to do."

Stemming from this folk theory, case managers believed the girls'
lives could be improved only by *moving* to "better," more structured
program environments. They suggested that more interactions with
staff would enable the girls to feel more cared for and would encourage successful behaviors. Decisions about program locations were
beyond the caseworkers' authority. Therefore, they could make such
suggestions unconstrained by practical limitations (including low
per diem rates from CYS and landlord prejudices). The caseworkers'
folk theory of change is supported by research. Peter Dreier, John
Mollenkopf, and Tom Swanstrom (2004: 70) report several studies
that indicate that when residents moved from "high-poverty ghet-
tos" to become "middle-class suburbanites," the new environment
had a "beneficial impact on people's sense of 'efficacy.' "

Evidence contradicts a culture-of-poverty model, as altered environments rapidly shift individual motivations and ways of being. As
James E. Rosenbaum, Lisa Reynolds, and Stefanie DeLuca have argued, "Places matter. The attributes of neighborhoods and the experiences provided by neighborhoods have profound effects on people's capabilities and their ideas about what they can accomplish"

(quoted in Dreier, Mollenkopf, and Swanstrom 2004: 70–71). Case managers understood that over time, limitations associated with unsafe SIL environments mediated youth's coping processes. Many clients agreed with their case managers. Repeatedly, they expressed their desire to move out of "the ghetto," raise their children in better neighborhoods, and expose the children to educational and extracurricular opportunities. Lack of safety restricted young mothers' identities. Clients lived in fear, felt uncared for by staff, and restricted their daily mobility. For instance, one client who walked me through her apartment a couple of days after the murder reenacted what she had done after hearing gunshots. With a panicked expression on her face, she showed me how she had moved her children into the bathroom. She pointed out her children's beds, which she had moved permanently from the bedroom to the living room. She did not want them sleeping next to the wall, which framed the central lounge where the young man had been murdered.

The program managers and the director were responsible for deciding where the program would be housed. Given the multiple ways structural constraints (outside their control) hindered movement, they justified keeping youth and children in the "community"—or the "ghetto," as youth referred to it. Program managers believed the program should support youth to become individually resilient, despite environmental obstacles. To protect their self-worth and sense of efficacy, the administrators tended to neutralize the effects of place. This enabled them to feel productive and useful in their roles.

Following the murder, I interviewed Beth, the SIL director. Her explanation echoed the responses of the program managers:

And that's why we look at the benefits of renting the way we do. The benefit is that we are not isolating the girls, that we are really having them live as part of a community. The problem is then we have to take all of the community issues, the roaches, the drugs, and everything else. . . . That's [the environment] where they are going to be. How do you go on with your life and keep looking forward rather than get tunneled or sidetracked by the stuff that's going on? . . . I mean the murder was really hard on everyone . . . but the reality is murders can happen anywhere. [Pause.]

Beth attempted to normalize a murder occurring at a program site. She believed the purpose of the program was to assist moms in becoming increasingly resilient individuals. Yet "looking forward," according to Beth, did not mean moving out of the urban "ghetto." Beth suggested that the SIL program was responsible for providing enough support to offset the challenges resulting from violence and an underresourced urban setting.

An upper-level CYS administrator echoed Beth's comment but also suggested that the mandate to "keep the kids in the community" created more challenges than officials generally recognized:

> Keep the kids in the community is another sort of value, which is kind of an absolute value, and we could argue whether it should be or not. . . . At the same time, it is complicated for these kids. Sometimes adhering to these values puts kids at risk—you know, in terms of just violence in the neighborhood, poor education in the neighborhood schools—so it is not as simple as having an ideology and trying to apply it. It is much more complicated. In general, it is a sound approach because if you pull kids out of their neighborhood for a year or year and a half, they have to come back at some point.

This administrator believed that these particular kids would end up living in unsafe, urban neighborhoods, again reflecting (and thus perpetuating) an assumption that mobility is limited for poor urban youth of color. Neither group of caseworkers or administrators mentioned a third possibility of political advocacy—collectively organizing to change the broader environment and reduce racial, economic, and social stratification. In other words, both groups' level of analysis rested in building individual resiliency either by transporting clients to "better" neighborhoods or by fostering resiliency within their marginalized communities. Through using folk theories, SIL staff members coped with the challenges they faced on the job. Caseworkers could explain why they were often unable to protect their clients and foster youth development. This could be blamed on the dangerous program environments. Program managers and the SIL director could justify keeping the program in the "inner city." These perspectives permitted caseworkers and officials to feel temporarily competent. Staff members' views prevented them from understanding and seeing how their decisions were restricted through structural inequalities based on race, class, gender, and age. These discrepancies are widespread in the child welfare system and across multiple sectors of society.

Individual beliefs about social change were never stagnant, and these shifted across time and space. A couple of years after my interview with Beth Spellman, we met for brunch. Our socializing was informal. During our conversation, Beth offered ideas about client improvement that echoed case managers' folk theories. She lamented sending clients to public housing high-rises, which she said were dead ends for the young families. She suggested that the families needed to move into better environments in order to get ahead. Beth was frustrated by the decline of programs such as Section 8, which enabled poor families to move into middle-class neighborhoods. Since we interacted socially, perhaps Beth did not feel the need to defend her position and sense of responsibility for the SIL program. Even as her comments seemed to contradict her earlier ideas, the shifting views make sense when we consider changing contexts and positions. The need to preserve one's identity and sense of competence is deeply connected to one's folk theory.

The Breakdown of the Familiar Zone

The murder threatened the program's familiar zones in two ways. First, it exposed the agency to additional scrutiny from its regulators (including the court and CYS) and the public (including the media). Familiar zones could exist only if authority figures could not see the spaces or the practices that took place there. Second, the murder disrupted the power hierarchy as mothers felt empowered to challenge the existence of the familiar zones. Mothers and case managers alike vocalized the dangers they faced in the program. Before the murder, expressions of dissent remained mostly within familiar zones. Clients repeatedly described instances of strangers banging on their doors late at night. SIL staff had full access to clients' apartments. Some mothers reported their panic when jolted from sleep by workers conducting surveillance and curfew checks. During these moments, mothers were uncertain whether an intruder was breaking in or a program official was entering the apartment. Many also said they feared walking the hallways or entering the building after dark.

As a public tragedy fractured "the facade of cohesion" (Scott 1990: 56), the hierarchy of positions became less rigid. Judges, CYS officials, and even clients held SIL program administrators accountable for their claim to provide safe SIL residences. Some youth used these safety claims to leverage access to alternative services. Two youth successfully directed their POs and CYS officials to pressure Visions into moving them to different residences (although clients were unclear whether these were safer).

For SIL program officials to continue receiving operational funds, they needed to demonstrate (or at least uphold an impression of) effective governance and service provision. During the staff meeting the Monday afternoon following the murder, the program managers' sense of panic was palpable as they attempted to maintain order. Administrators were afraid of liability for the dangerous conditions in the program. They sought to unify voices of dissent and preserve the public face of the program. An adult female resident of the apartment building distributed a letter to the media, local government, and SIL program administrators. I did not get a copy of the letter but an administrator reported that it presented the many problems associated with the apartment building. The resident admonished the administrators for housing a program for young families in such a dangerous location. The SIL administrators advised case managers not to speak to the media and to direct all inquiries to the executive director of the agency. She alone would be responsible for the program's public profile.

The murder exposed the high level of violence at a program site, and participants' acts of impression management became largely futile. Harsh criticism followed. Officials from CYS and two judges admonished SIL case managers and administrators, threatening to discontinue Visions' SIL contract. SIL staff found it difficult to justify the integrity of the program. When I accompanied Tomeka and her infant son to court early one morning, I observed firsthand the judge's harsh reprimand. Tomeka and I, along with her son, mother, and PO, walked to the front of the courtroom and approached the judge, who was white and female and appeared to be in her early forties.

This was a routine judicial review. After the PO, who was African American, introduced each of us, the judge asked immediately whether the SIL program had moved Tomeka from the Evergreen building. Her PO answered that she would be moved that same afternoon to an apartment on a higher floor in the Evergreen building. The PO attempted to justify the program's decision. Because the program had a large number of residents living at Evergreen, it was taking a long time to move everyone. The judge was astonished that the agency would keep a program in such an unsafe building. She reminded us that if anything were to happen to a client, the agency would be shut down immediately. The judge solicited Tomeka directly, asking whether she felt safe in the SIL program. Tomeka quickly replied, "No," hesitated, then turned to her PO and asked, "Would you feel safe?" The PO reminded Tomeka that the judge had asked her the question. Tomeka restated, "No, I do not feel safe." The judge appeared genuinely concerned and professed how sorry she was that she could not move Tomeka to a different agency. There were no other openings.

With a simple question, Tomeka highlighted the class-based inequalities in her "care," implying that her PO would expect better conditions if she were in Tomeka's position. This made her PO uncomfortable, and apparently the judge as well. In that moment, Tomeka forced the public officials to acknowledge the discrepancy between the child welfare's mission and her reality. Even the judge's decision making was constrained by the larger child welfare system. The system did not invest in enough viable, safe residential options to support the number of children and youth in need.

Despite the warnings issued by judges and officials, the SIL program retained its contract. Soon after data collection for this study ended, I learned that CYS prevented the SIL program from accepting new participants until it met particular requirements.[3] Several months later, CYS allowed the SIL program to resume accepting new clients, although the program changed its structure. It shifted from three main apartment sites to scattered apartments at multiple sites throughout the city. While beyond the scope of this study, it is important to determine whether program improvements tend to follow public scrutiny, or whether scrutiny is fleeting and inconsequential.

Conclusion

Familiar zones perpetuated service inconsistencies and oppressive conditions and allowed participants to adapt creatively within a "moral underground." When policymakers, researchers, and the public fail to acknowledge the informal program lives of youth, structural problems remain invisible. Paying attention to the formation of familiar zones increases our understanding of the informal strategies used by youth and their caseworkers, as well as the reasons why they cannot freely resist systemic barriers. Officials and the public continue to require superhuman efforts from disenfranchised youth, ones we would not require from our own children.

When familiar zones broke down, individuals across the child welfare hierarchy acknowledged the unjust conditions experienced by the same youth the system was mandated to protect. Acknowledgment of harsh realities does not necessarily lead to system restructuring. The tendency to blame the individual (whether this is the mother, the case manager, or the administrator) can limit change, because blaming fails to promote broad critique or system restructuring. Such a tendency also jeopardizes investment in child welfare systems and governance. When familiar zones are exposed to the public, participants gain freedom to communicate dissenting standpoints. Exposure may cause officials and the public to openly acknowledge the reality of oppression within the system. That acknowledgment may provide opportunities for deliberation, dialogue, and strategizing to promote improved conditions of care. It is a social justice concern that programs such as SIL be improved (not eliminated) so that adolescent mothers and their children receive stable and supportive contexts of care.

Not only did mothers navigate dangerous and inequitable program terrains; they were also caught trying to make sense of conflicting accounts of themselves. In chapter 3, I focus on the circulating and contradictory representations of adolescent mothers and how youth negotiated these narratives. Through conflicting narratives, urban systems and officials set up infeasible goals for these youth and then made it impossible for them to reach the benchmarks.

CHAPTER THREE

The Real Responsibility Is on You!

The Self-Sufficiency Trap

Anisa, a nineteen-year-old mother of two young girls, provided an apt analogy for the disconnection she experienced between an official's expectations for her identity work and her own desires and choices:

> It's like he [the CYS worker] . . . tells me I have to paint this wall. "You've got to paint it. You've got to paint it." I mean, "Paint it or else this will happen to you." And I'm looking at him like, "I'm not painting this because I'm not good at it." I'm letting him know right then and there that I'm not good at painting. . . . You know, it's my choice. "Can I do something that I'm good at? Can I, you know, mop the floors?" I'm good at mopping the floors. . . . And he would say like, "No, I said paint the wall." [Anisa laughs.] OK, I will give it a try.

Anisa felt pressured and threatened by her caseworker's notion of compliance; she wanted to demonstrate compliance in more nuanced ways. The SIL program and its officials privileged fixed ideas about how a youth in care should achieve independence. A myth of self-sufficiency compromised interconnected, caring relationships between participants. I repeatedly witnessed tears of frustration or outbursts of anger as youth felt extreme pressure to prove they deserved assistance. For youth entangled in the child welfare system, organizational barriers and assumptions about their dependency compromised their personal power. Aimee Cox (2007) notes the ways institutions and the public sphere identify low-income black girls, ways that limit the youths' participation in their own representations.

This chapter shows how stigmatized conceptions of youth contributed to shortsighted programs and policies, as well as to a general ethos of fear. Stigma narratives hindered the creation of communities of care among young families and their providers. Through contemporary governance, social policies for children and youth align according to the logic of the market. Agencies are caught between the competing objectives of cutting costs and providing needed services (Blau and Abramovitz 2010). Officials apply common models to ration services and to justify which individuals should receive help. In the first model, government provides services to "deserving," poor individuals amenable to rehabilitation (see, e.g., Katz 1989, 2001). In the second, government provides services to poor women who are victims of harsh circumstances or abuse (see, e.g., Haney 2010). Scholars discuss these models largely in reference to adult poor women, and there is a notable absence of discourse concerning children and youth. In practice, I found that policymakers and caseworkers in the child welfare system commonly applied these same models to youth.

A third model coexists with and often trumps the other two: government officials assess relative risk to decide who should receive services. Officials determined whether a youth's dependency was likely to result in her being harmed and if so, whether the government should provide services and oversight. However, officials sometimes used risk management to cease services for a client. If a teenage client's *behavior* put the SIL program at risk, then officials tended to discharge her. Needless to say, workers justified providing services or withholding them by drawing on assumptions about the value or danger of a particular youth.

Youth in the child welfare system sometimes perceive themselves as infantilized, particularly in the negotiation of services and resources. In other contexts, officials expect these same youth to make the independent decisions of an adult. What ideologies inform expectations attached to youth categories? And how do these shift across settings? Narratives from youth in child welfare systems contribute to and complicate scholarly discussions of gender, poverty, race, and adult welfare systems (see, e.g., Collins and Meyer 2010; Katz 2001; Kingfisher 2002; Morgen, Acker, and Weigt 2010; and Ridzi 2009).

Performing Victimization, Performing Responsibility

Identity is always negotiated in context (Gee 2000). Youth perform identity "bids" through their performances and officials use their power to recognize or discount such bids (Gee 2000). In SIL I found that even when moms were perceptive in managing impressions, the necessity to perform according to regulators' standards compromised open, flexible, and fluid selves. As James Scott (1990: 35) suggests, identity performances must be "approved by the dominant." For these SIL youth, "the dominant" included official gatekeepers but also the ideologies that required them to earn their own care. A handful of "successful" youth came to be *known* as hard workers, good students, and good mothers. However, officials perceived many youth as poor decision makers, deviant, or unsalvageable. Clients attempted to present themselves as "needy" and requiring services but also as deserving persons capable of self-transformation. They could not appear too self-sufficient or they would risk losing assistance. Youth navigated this perilous representational terrain. Narratives, which focused on client attributes and accountability alone, removed attention from the structural changes needed to make the SIL program and child welfare system affirm (rather than undermine) the dignity of youth and their young families.

Caseworkers would discuss at length a client's disposition and perceived ability to change. However, these deliberations were often secondary to managing risk. As we have seen, the program did not tend to discharge clients for breaking program rules alone; instead, it did so when landlords, CYS regulators, judges, or the media identified problem behaviors. The program's risk management procedures shaped clients' identity performances.

Kelley, a nineteen-year-old dependent mother, provides a compelling case that shows how youth attempted to negotiate a liminal representation terrain in a risk management context. Kelley was in immediate danger of being discharged from the program because of the company she kept. CYS allowed youth to remain in the child welfare system on extensions after they turned eighteen and up until their twenty-first birthdays. The extended support was meant to encourage successful transitions into self-sufficient adulthood. The state's legislation put the onus on the youth to request continued services while in school or treatment. However, in practice, youth did not control these decisions. Youth workers recommended a client's extension to the judge, and ultimately the judge made the call. Extensions were uncertain for youth because the federal government did not mandate their care. Since Kelley was on an extension, she would likely lose all child welfare services if discharged from SIL.

Purportedly as a result of "issues with a boyfriend who is a known drug dealer" and "traffic" coming in and out of her apartment, the landlords required that Kelley be removed from their building. As a program manager, I experienced firsthand just how difficult it was to relocate and to find landlords willing to lease large numbers of apartments to the SIL program. On several occasions, landlords either threatened or actually refused to continue leasing apartments because of a client's purported involvement in drug transactions on their premises. Whether landlords based their claims on real evidence or prejudiced assumptions was not of consequence. They had full authority over their leases, and they often used their power strategically to their advantage. SIL staff complained repeatedly about landlords who used threats of eviction to make the program pay for site damages. According to the staff, landlords often blamed program participants for damages that the latter did not cause.

Therefore, once Kelley was identified as a "problem," the program was vulnerable to repercussions. Kelley had experienced trouble once before at a different apartment site, at which point the SIL program had moved her to the location in question. Her situation was not unusual. I was aware of a number of clients the SIL program had moved from one site to another (because of an identified problem). Around a crowded conference table at the SIL program's administrative office, Kelley presented her "case" to seven SIL staff members, including Beth Spellman, the SIL director, and six caseworkers. She would need to convince them to allow her to remain in the program. I was present and tape-recorded the discussion, with Kelley's permission. However, she granted this permission under particularly stressful conditions—Kelley was in a vulnerable position and may not have felt comfortable denying my request. I am sensitive to these circumstances. I hope that including this vignette will elucidate Kelley's aptitude in negotiating her identities. This routine service context shows how individualized narratives challenged clients' resiliencies and made structural problems invisible.

Several months before this meeting, Kelley had lost custody of her daughter. I am unaware of the specific reasons, but this outcome was not unusual for clients in the SIL program. When mothers were under court regulation, they experienced increased scrutiny and surveillance within the system. This often resulted in the loss of custody of their children. Kelley had recently received visitation privileges. If discharged, she would lose what little ground she had gained in getting her daughter back. She was therefore desperate to remain in the program. Beth Spellman said to Kelley, "OK. You're on," and Kelley responded with the following:

> OK. The most I can say is that . . . I have to grow. I have to learn how to lead a life. The only reason why I can see myself going through what I went through is because I have no family. . . . Meaning that if I get put out of here, I have no place to go but a shelter. [Her voice is shaking.] . . . I really miss my daughter so much. [She starts to cry.] . . . I will try my best to do anything I can to get my daughter back. It's just I've been around the wrong people. . . . It's just like I should have paid more attention to who I was hanging around, who I was involved with. . . . I mean I take, I take the blame for everything.

Later in the session, Beth asked Kelley, "Tell me, what could possibly be different if we give you another chance?" Kelley responded,

> The only difference that can be made is through me. And that's my company. I understand that if I do get another chance, I don't want to know nobody. I'm going to continue doing what I've been doing. Go to my school. Go to my work. And doing what I got to do to get my daughter back.

Kelley was clearly aware of the staff's expectation that she should take personal responsibility for her behavior and should disengage from her social life. Kelley was very deferential and accepted blame for her misconduct. She played the role of a respectful and remorseful client. Yet she argued for her continued involvement in the program by highlighting her "endangerment" (Tilton 2010) and lack of family support. To justify her assistance, Kelley knew she needed to enact the role of a victim. Also, she was cognizant of the staff's low opinion of the young men in her environment. The staff members did not discourage Kelley's unrealistic plan to isolate herself. Their silence supported, at least tacitly, their low regard for Kelley's community. Their silence also confirmed that self-segregation was the only feasible approach to avoid social and environmental challenges. Yet seclusion directly contradicts an interdependent understanding of youth development, which requires connecting with peers, exploring romantic relationships, and finding acceptance in one's community (Erikson 1999; Nakkula and Toshalis 2008; Spencer 2006). In part of the encounter not quoted, Kelley tried to provide context for her "bad" decision making. She explained the lack of personal freedom she experienced during her childhood. Kelley saw herself as having been a "slave" in her uncle's home. She was trying to learn how to lead an "independent" life but implied that she lacked models and appropriate knowledge from which to draw.

As Kelley left the room in tears, the staff informed her that she would be notified about their decision the following day. After Kelley exited, a caseworker offered the following assessment:

> I mean she was crying like that with me. I mean, she speaks well. . . .
> As a person, I like her. But she is weak in that man field. . . . She
> was dealing with men in their twenties, thirties. And she was at
> work. And she is a worker. . . . But they have her door keys. . . .
> Some [clients] will cuss you out and say all kinds of things, but
> she doesn't. [Other caseworkers agreed, and a one caseworker
> said, "She hasn't been disrespectful."]

According to the caseworkers, Kelley was unable to act on her stated intention to "change." Kelley floundered in the ambiguity of conflicting expectations. Staff considered her to be a deserving and likeable person, as well as a hard worker. The caseworkers viewed her as lacking self-efficacy in other areas: she was unable to make appropriate relationship decisions. On the one hand, Kelley had to embody victimization in order to "bid" herself as a youth who deserved and needed services. She tried to justify her past mistakes, highlighting the victimization, neglect, and abuse that she had experienced. On the other hand, Kelley had to demonstrate that she was capable of making responsible decisions. The divide between victim and self-efficacious identities was a tenuous one, putting Kelley in an impossible situation.

Public and private gender orders compromised Kelley's agency. Power worked in complicated ways through institutional inequalities and a matrix of gender, class, race, and age divides. The older men who inhabited SIL apartments often controlled clients physically, economically, and socially. These forms of control undermined the program's authority. Some caseworkers offered advice to moms who dealt with ongoing abuse; these exchanges occurred in the shadows (in program familiar zones). These men did not officially belong in the program. Therefore, policies and program interventions did not directly address the high level of domestic abuse experienced by many clients in program settings.

These ecological conditions contributed to Kelley's "choices," but the identity expectations that Kelley felt compelled to exhibit did not allow her to speak about ongoing constraints on her freedom. The staff agreed that Kelley should be discharged because she had been moved once before and continued to make bad decisions about male companions. As we saw in chapter 2, staff members were aware of the environmental challenges that SIL program locations caused, and they knew that these settings influenced youth behaviors. However, these perceptions did not ultimately factor into their decisions. Staff members needed to manage risk while working in an imperfect system. Client responsibility discourses were normative and created an ideology of "common sense" (Ridzi 2009) enacted by all participants—youth and caseworkers alike. Staff members drew on client responsibility and irresponsibility narratives in an effort to assert their authority. In the process, these client-focused narratives enabled staff members to ignore their own ineffectiveness and vulnerabilities.

It is not that discourses of self-sufficiency and individual betterment have no place in a SIL program for youth and their children.

Youth wanted to achieve independence—to provide for their children and to lead a "worthy" life. Programs should be designed to support youth in meeting their goals. Clear communication about mutual expectations is also important. But a myopic focus on these individual conditions alone is detrimental because it ignores collective lives and broader conditions that confine individual decision making.

I later learned that Beth disregarded the group consensus and decided to keep Kelley in the program. She moved her once again, to the third apartment site. The day after the deliberation, Beth met one on one with Kelley in her office. She suggested to me that Kelley suffered sexual and psychological abuse in her uncle's home, and she wanted to give her one last chance to be successful in the program. Kelley's behavior would not be known to the landlord at the third apartment site. The program would no longer face an immediate threat of eviction. Even so, the environment at this third site was similar to the location in question. Would different programming be put in place to support Kelley so that the same predicament would not recur? Different programming would likely not be possible because of ongoing staff shortages and structural challenges. These events occurred near the completion of my fieldwork, and I was unable to follow up on what happened to Kelley.

Interactions between other clients and staff drew on similar individualizing discourses. In fact, the SIL program had a common format for formal deliberations. This format was unwritten and learned through social interactions. Formal deliberations involved at least one high-level official (e.g., the SIL program director, a judge, PO, or CYS worker) in a high-stakes decision (e.g., whether a client should be discharged from the program). These negotiations occurred in formal program spaces rather than in familiar zones. Either staff pushed clients to accept blame or youth took the initiative in claiming responsibility for their "failures." Youth also tried to demonstrate the will and ability to improve their behaviors, often justifying past transgressions by citing histories of victimization. In the process of making decisions, officials referred to a client's attributes or her ability or inability to make responsible decisions. While discussions were consequential, they were informed by risk management and material conditions. For example, if an apartment at a different location had been unavailable, Kelley would likely have been discharged (in spite of the director's sympathy for her). These formal negotiations were never completely deterministic. Kelley's perseverance and self-efficacy were also important. Had she not followed up in a private meeting and convinced Beth to let her try again, she would likely have been discharged.

Mediating Care

I share another formal deliberation. Tomeka negotiated her identities in a manner similar to Kelley; however, workers responded differently to her identity "bids." Neither a regulator nor a landlord had noticed Tomeka's "problem" behavior. Since program officials did not experience an external risk, the backdrop for negotiation was friendlier and outwardly supportive. I introduced Tomeka, a nineteen-year-old delinquent mother, in chapter 2 when she was compelled to attend the agency's GED class with her baby. Since Tomeka was also on an extension, she was at risk of losing all child welfare provisions. She asked me to accompany her to the meeting, and I drove her to the SIL administrative office. She had provoked an altercation at the agency's GED class, and SIL officials required her to attend a formal deliberation. Jane, the SIL program manager; Ramona, her GED teacher; her PO; and her therapist were waiting in the conference room when we arrived.

When Jane asked Tomeka to explain what had happened, Tomeka said she had come to school very frustrated on the morning of the incident. She added that she truly regretted her actions. Supposedly, Tomeka had attempted to strike a woman who attended the GED class after the woman expressed frustration with Tomeka for talking loudly on the telephone. Tomeka exclaimed that the woman had pushed her "nerves." In a nagging tone, she enacted the woman saying, "I'm trying to get my education." Tomeka explained that Ramona had jumped in and restrained her before she could actually hit the woman. Ramona acknowledged that Tomeka did not resist her hold. Tomeka's PO argued that this indicated Tomeka's ability to control herself when she chose to do so. Both Jane and Ramona believed that they had trusting, open relationships with Tomeka. Jane emphasized that Tomeka could confide in her if she was having a bad day, and Ramona offered special classroom accommodations for when Tomeka felt upset.

I had learned on the car ride over something that was not revealed during the deliberation: Tomeka was pregnant again, and, even in this condition, her boyfriend continued to beat her. The stress from this trauma likely had shaped her frustration and behavior that day in the classroom. However, during the formal deliberation, Tomeka did not mention these circumstances or why she was frustrated on the day of the incident. Although staff members clearly cared about Tomeka, domestic abuse was not discussed in this formal setting. The PO concluded the meeting by encouraging Tomeka to draw on supportive staff members; she declared, "You know I love you, but I have to be honest with you. This is it!" The PO looked directly at Tomeka and continued, "The next place for you will be a locked [penal] facility, and CYS will be waiting to take your son into custody. You need to get it together!" Tomeka was at a metaphoric fork in the road: she could fail, lose her child, and get incarcerated or she could put herself on a path to self-sufficiency purportedly through her own self-control, personal strength, and willingness to take guidance from SIL staff. Child welfare programs like SIL justify their existence to the public only when clients meet measurable self-sufficiency indicators. Tomeka managed her identity and tried to appear capable of self-rehabilitation and self-sufficiency.

It is possible that some of the staff knew about Tomeka's abuse, as I did. Yet we conspired in silence during the official performance. In retrospect, I believe this conspiracy was unexamined, the result of a culture of fear. Clients revealed experiences of violence and domestic abuse to staff members in conversations in program familiar zones, when program residency and child custody issues were not at stake. In the preceding vignette, we adults and Tomeka worked together to fashion Tomeka as capable of positive and productive personal growth. It was normative and simply "common sense" to do so during a formal deliberation. But the adults represented Tomeka's future path as one that Tomeka would choose on her own. The players did not address factors that impeded Tomeka's free agency. She was under the violent control of her boyfriend. Since Tomeka did not actually strike the woman, the officials did not feel compelled to punish her. Also, Tomeka's respectful and remorseful attitude helped her cause.

Similarly, staff perceived Kelley as a respectful and well-liked client, but in contrast to their approach to Tomeka, they did not tell Kelley this directly. They waited until she left the room. Kelley posed an immediate risk to the program, while Tomeka did not, and staff needed to discursively justify their discharge decision to Kelley.

During her formal negotiation, I wonder whether Tomeka perceived that the staff cared for her. I regret that I didn't ask her directly. It was not safe for her to disclose her trauma because she did not want her PO to perceive her as too damaged or a lost cause. Such a disclosure could have resulted in discharge from the program—particularly because her care was not mandated. Underfunded policies, rationed services, shortsighted conceptions of youth, and a culture of fear limited caseworkers' and young mothers' ability to form collective bonds of support.

The power dynamics during official exchanges required youth to fashion themselves as public spectacles (Farley 2002)—they pointed out their own mistakes, responsibilities, and desire to change. Staff watched these shows and evaluated them but did not disclose how they (or program contexts) also contributed to a youth's predicament. Stylized and ritualized performances are common across U.S. rehabilitation programs. Performances become a form of public shaming, ostensibly meant to encourage clients to reform their characters (Haney 2010). Frank Ridzi (2009: 17) suggests that in the late 1980s and early 1990s, "a new thesis emerged of a stereotypically black urban 'underclass' . . . in need of 'tough love' attempts to shock them out of a 'culture of dependency.' "

Lynne Haney (2010) studied residential programs for delinquent adolescent mothers and adult mothers and found similar spectacle-making processes at work. The act of shaming the individual client distracts everyone involved from the deeper processes of marginalization, which position poor young women of color as objects and officials as moral judges. Hierarchies of power are enacted in ways that become common sense. Participants focus on performance qualities rather than openly discuss experiences of violence and injustice. Further, participants are distracted from considering the ways bureaucratic systems construct youth (and their workers) as "failures." What would it mean to transgress the boundaries of these "therapeutic" constructions? As a precondition, each participant would need to be conscious of the socially constructed nature of the client spectacle and the worker judge. She or he would need to feel safe to transgress these boundaries. What forms of connection and collaboration might result if staff members and clients jointly discussed their vulnerabilities and desires for change?

Next, I look more closely at conceptions of youth in the child welfare system and draw on interviews with a range of child welfare officials. Officials' interpretations of youth policies reflected problematic and fractured narratives.

Dilemmas of Representation

Within the SIL program, youth received services through one of two court-ordered pathways: they were adjudicated as either dependent or delinquent. Officials and youth alike understood that these simplistic legal categorizations, "delinquent" and "dependent," were not mutually exclusive. Both groups of mothers lived in the same apartment buildings at the three SIL locations, and the SIL program oversaw the two groups in the same way. Yet youth experienced unequal treatment within the broader system. Delinquent youth received fewer services, experienced additional surveillance from their POs, and dealt with greater stigma. Many of the delinquent teens were abused and abandoned, as were the dependent moms. Workers were quick to mention that many dependent mothers engaged in delinquent acts but were lucky enough not to get caught. Depending on which system identified them first, youth received a label of *dependent* or *delinquent*, and these labels mediated the pathways open to them.

Both groups of youth survived interpersonal and structural violence. Rather than perceiving youth as resilient, officials more often understood them as unfortunate, vulnerable victims or as deviant, damaged teens. Representations had an impact, as policies and practices perpetuated shortsighted stereotypes about poor, black, adolescent mothers (see, e.g., Luttrell 2003; Pillow 2004; Rhode and Lawson 1993; and Solinger 1992). Media representations and trends in public policies *make* young single black mothers blameworthy for poverty and other woes in black communities (Katz 2001; Kunzel 1993; Pearce 1993; Phoenix 1993; Solinger 1992).[1] Jennifer Tilton (2010) characterizes the tensions between the dual, dominant youth representations that circulate globally, captured in the title of her book *Dangerous or Endangered?* Youth of color "have long been linked with other symbolic associations—criminality and sexuality—that have undermined their ability to make claims on the state" (10). I too found that policies and negotiations on the ground reflected these representational tensions.

In an interview I conducted with a middle-aged CYS official, he highlighted his clients' endangerment. This official believed that teen parenthood resulted from the victimization of children. In particular, he noted that family situations forced many children to take on adult roles at young ages. He lamented the "impact of drugs on our community," noting that crack "seems to take away the maternal instinct." According to the official, addicted parents meant "a lot of kids raising themselves" and, presumably, becoming parents themselves at young ages. He noted how violence had intensified since he had been a youth. A black male, he had grown up in the same neighborhood as many of his clients. He broadened his discussion when he mentioned a bigger "societal thing," in which "the culture exploits girls. . . . The sexualizing of babies and children has become just an expected feature of our life now. Children are exposed to that, they *become* that."

Another high-level official referred to narratives of "endangerment," as he explained the dilemmas faced by delinquent teen mothers. He acknowledged that "there are more girls in the system now." Even though they did not commit "hard-core" crimes, they were caught in the system for lengthier periods than boys. Girls lacked homes and faced more dependency issues caused by abuse and neglect. He explained:

Now, they're not delinquent. They are mothers with no resources, no ability to make do for themselves and with the stigma of an arrest. And now they got children. And many times the boys or young men they are dealing with are not positive parents themselves. . . . Now they got these babies, but they don't have the wherewithal to get themselves out of trouble because now they missed schooling. . . . So they have really set themselves up for a long life of struggle. . . . But here you have a child who was basically abandoned herself. Now she has a child, and that's tough.

Even as this official presented himself as generally sympathetic to the plight of young mothers, he drew on conflicting discourses. He moved from representing the girls as victims to placing the onus for a "life of struggle" on the individuals themselves. A middle-aged female PO also emphasized victimization and external barriers when describing SIL youth:

Because by the time you get to independent living, you've either been sexually abused, abandoned, hooked up with the wrong guy, you know, just so many outside factors, that I always think, the *Girl, Interrupted.* That's what I think of my girls, their life is interrupted.

These types of narratives were not unusual when caseworkers and upper-level officials described their "endangered" clients. While these discourses destigmatized youth behaviors, they also downplayed the self-efficacy of these adolescents. Many officials believed that "outside factors" had led to the dual "victimization" and "delinquency" of their clients. Youth also commonly used stories about their victimization to justify their "problem" behaviors.

Caseworkers and officials were not always sympathetic to the challenging circumstances that informed youth actions. Sometimes these same workers treated clients as dangerous and conniving. James Scott (1990) suggests that officials attribute "lying" behavior not to the effect of *power* but to "inborn" and "innate" characteristics of subordinate groups. When a market-driven system of governance rations essential resources, individuals strategize to get their needs and desires met. Clients were not free to assert preferences, and officials often communicated mixed messages. The system did not reward youth who failed to meet particular educational, parenting, and life-skills standards, and the system undersupported the youth in reaching expectations. As a consequence, youth managed their presentations of self in ways that were not always factual. Often officials considered them to be manipulative. It would be unfair and inappropriate for officials to expect them to be otherwise, given the high stakes, unavailable resources, and lack of comprehensive support. Contradictory and shifting understandings of youth promoted narrow interpretations of child welfare policies. Next, I explore this assertion through a particular child welfare policy: the board extension.

Board Extension Policy: Inconsistent Interpretations

CYS allowed some youth to remain in the child welfare system on a board extension after turning age eighteen and up until their twenty-first birthdays. The legislation mandated that youth receive support until the completion of their "course." Alisa Field (2004: 209) interprets "course of treatment" as including a range of independent living services to assist youth in "growing up." However, I observed that officials granted extensions based on *school attendance only*. Mothers, caseworkers, and administrators all told me that CYS providers and judges regularly threatened to discharge youth not attending an educational program. Field acknowledged that many child agencies violated this mandate by discharging youth immediately at age eighteen. Or officials applied a restricted interpretation of this clause, which led a client to be discharged immediately after completing an educational program. Immediate discharge did not allow youth the time to work and build savings to support themselves and their children on their own.

Inconsistent interpretation and application of this board extension policy contributed to an atmosphere of fear and threat. For instance, Mr. Jones, a top-level, white CYS administrator, told me the following:

> There is a board extension policy here, which we're going to kind of examine in light of the growing numbers of kids coming into our system at fifteen or sixteen and see if that can be modified in any way that makes sense. Ideally, it would be terrific if the federal government were . . . to support these kids until they are

twenty-one but they don't, so we had our own board extension policy that *doesn't always get applied evenly and interpreted consistently*. It allows us to support kids in dependent care until they are age twenty-one if they are engaged in some form of education. What we run into now, for example, you know advocates for those kids would interpret that as an *entitlement* rather than something that certain groups of kids sort of *earn* or *deserve*. . . . We say it's [a board extension,] not an entitlement. We say we choose to invest in kids and continue to invest in kids, for example, who have come up through our system, who have done well in foster care for five or ten years. We're not going to kick them out the door when they're eighteen. . . . But when older kids are coming into our system at sixteen and seventeen, *are they as entitled or deserving* or can we program for those kids beyond eighteen? And it's also an issue of budget. You know, what we can afford, we can fund. [My emphasis]

Mr. Jones drew on a model of the deserving poor to justify service provision. He appropriated the model to classify different groups of children as more or less worthy. Given the lack of support from the federal government, local systems were forced to cut costs and ration resources. After a youth turned eighteen, Mr. Jones explained, continuation of child welfare support depended on the youth's meeting two conditions: growing up in foster care and participating in school. He implied that teenagers could be manipulative and take advantage of public resources. He understood young children to be truly disadvantaged and regarded CYS services as essential. Mr. Jones perceived the financing of programs such as SIL as an investment. Because of government deficits, the child welfare system could invest in only kids who grew up in the system and who had already proved themselves worthy.

Mr. Jones reported that in 2001, CYS served 28 percent of children who were fourteen years old and above and that in January 2005, 40 percent of children in care were in this age bracket. The child welfare system increasingly provided services to older youth. Teens were an expensive population because they generally did not return home. Beth Spellman, the SIL director, contested that youth were denied services because of lack of funding. She maintained that money shortages reflected the broader public's perception of poor black adolescent females as unworthy of financial investment.

> Some of it, you know, I think can really be around people's judgment of who the girls are and what they deserve and don't deserve. I mean that is sometimes an issue that these girls sometimes aren't so deserving and why are we, you know, spending our dollars on blah blah blah.

These narratives shaped the practices of service provision and compromised an ethos of care. Each official viewed the requirements for a board extension differently. Youth worried endlessly about whether they would retain their SIL residences, especially because caseworker turnover was high.

The next vignette illustrates the ways officials' restrictive preconceptions actually disenfranchised youth. The case I present here is representative of the many youth who are turned away from the child welfare system and remain in the shadows.

Keeping Youth Out

One morning at the SIL administrative office, Jane, a program manager, asked if I could do her a favor. Jane proposed that I call CYS and advocate for Denise, who had been homeless for the past year and was living (unofficially) with Tamara, a SIL client. Denise was the mother of a three-year-old daughter. Often program staff members and clients asked me to assist with a variety of tasks and service negotiations. Participants were widely aware of my prior role as a SIL practitioner. I readily accepted Jane's request and after a brief conversation with the two friends, I called the CYS screening worker.

I was surprised when the CYS worker assessed (over the phone) whether this seventeen-year-old mother required further CYS investigation and services. Denise and Tamara sat next to each other at a secondhand conference table, and I stood adjacent to them with the telephone. The CYS worker refused my request that she meet in person with the youth, so I served as the intermediary. I tried to present Denise's case as deserving attention. Yet the CYS worker was unyielding in her perception of the youth as conniving. My frustration grew as she continued to discount every aspect of Denise's experience.

A pattern of interactions organized the conversation. The worker would ask questions to determine where Denise and her child should live, followed by my relaying Denise's responses. After each suggestion, Denise would clarify why the worker's idea was infeasible and the worker would discount her reply. For example, Denise responded that she could not return to her ninety-eight-year-old great-grandmother's home because she and her three-year-old daughter would burden the elderly woman. The worker viewed Denise through an adult lens; she believed this seventeen-year-old mother should assist the great-grandmother. Even after discovering that CYS had investigated an incident between Denise and her mother, the worker continued to push for Denise to return to her mother's home. The worker also asked for information about Denise's father and the father of Denise's daughter. Denise responded that she knew nothing about her own father and that her child's father was in prison. In reaction to the worker's question about why her child's father was locked up, Denise quickly replied, "Drugs." Tamara shook her head with a look of disgust and whispered something inaudible to Denise.

After this cursory exchange, the worker asked for Denise's mother's phone number so she could get "her side of the story." Then the worker ended the conversation. Communication between Denise and the CYS worker seemed flawed from the start. As an intermediary, I created a distinct boundary. Repeatedly, the worker attempted to discover resources she believed the young mother was hiding.

In retrospect, I understood that the screening worker's goal was not to connect with Denise or appreciate the ways she had suffered. Because of Denise's age, seventeen, the goal of saving public monies dominated any objective to provide care. To echo Mr. Jones, youth in Denise's position were not worth "investment," and officials viewed them as destined to perpetuate a cycle of poverty and abuse (see, e.g., Rutman et al. 2002). The screening worker's perception of Denise was in accord with dominant narratives about conniving, unruly teens who refused to get along with their parents. The worker discounted any potentially abusive circumstances in this teenager's parental "home." She expected Denise, like so many other youth in similar situations, to possess the independent qualities of an adult. The worker and the system ignored the vulnerabilities of adolescence and the normative developmental need for continued parental (or surrogate parental) involvement (Spencer et al. 2003).

It is likely that the screening worker operated under significant constraints not obvious during the conversation. These barriers probably shaped the ways she perceived Denise. As Mr. Jones mentioned, the system was flooded with growing numbers of youth. CYS administrators may have pressured this screening worker to scrutinize youth referrals. All the officials I spoke with seemed acutely aware of the limited funds available for CYS services. The screening worker was likely inundated with many more requests concerning children in need than the system had funding to support. Her preconceived notions about Denise may have been a way for her to cope. Irrespective of the worker's circumstances, her approach to Denise's case was cursory and discounting.

After I hung up, the three of us continued to discuss the situation. Tamara asked why the evaluator needed the information about the baby's father and added, "If he's not involved, he's not involved!" Denise needed to present herself as both in need of and deserving of services. She disclosed particular aspects of her life so that the CYS worker could ascertain whether she met the criteria for the court to order her as dependent. These criteria should be based on evidence of neglect, abuse, truancy, and parental incapacity. Tamara's interrogation seemed fitting and also revealed her sense of efficacy. She was well aware that this worker had abused her authority. Knowing *why* Denise's child's father was incarcerated did not help the worker establish whether Denise met the criteria for dependency. The worker felt at liberty to ask such a question, which highlights her sense of entitlement to Denise's private life. Determining a youth's eligibility for CYS services was in fact highly subjective. During this part of the assessment, the worker was clearly paternalistic. She perceived Denise as a child obligated to answer her questions. Paternalistic assumptions were common across interactions between officials and clients.

The worker relied on dual representations of Denise. She viewed her as a manipulative, adultlike individual when she attempted to justify why Denise should not receive services. She perceived her as a childlike dependent without rights to privacy when she questioned Denise's circumstances. Nancy Lesko (1995) notes that adolescent mothers deal with the "slippery" discourses of independence and dependency and that the public views them as being both too autonomous and too dependent. The worker did not personally experience accountability or scrutiny. Multiple, disconnected levels of child welfare administration meant the whims of individual officials superseded standards of client care.

Denise believed that her mother would tell the worker that she could live with her but that nothing would actually change and she would remain homeless. Denise expressed how difficult it had been for her because her mother had not provided a "single dime" since the birth of Denise's baby. Because of their strained relationship, Denise was unable to get on her mother's welfare case. Her situation was even more precarious because she was too young to get her own welfare case and her child's father could not provide support. Tamara claimed that Denise's situation with her mother was as dire as her own. Since Tamara had been in the system since she was a young child, she believed it was easier for her to receive services. This disparity reflects Mr. Jones's comment that the system was biased in favor of young children. Before leaving for the day, I gave Denise my phone number and told her I was willing to help her find services. I never heard from Denise again.

Denise fell through the cracks of a multitudinous network of governing entities, and she struggled without public support. Her age placed her in a particularly liminal location. The government considered her neither a full adult nor a child. She did not fall neatly into a particular system for public assistance. As a seventeen-year-old mother who had been abandoned by her own mother, she struggled to survive with her young daughter. Field (2004) interprets the state's legislation: the court should adjudicate a sixteen- or seventeen-year-old dependent if a youth requests services and meets the definition of a dependent child. Field continues: "Youth who cannot return home, or who have no home to return to, for example, meet the definition of dependency up to reaching the age of 18. Courts must enforce the child welfare agency's responsibility to these youth. . . . Often these older youth are most in need of assistance of the court and child welfare agency because they are turned away by agencies which serve the adult population. Without assistance of the child welfare system these minors will likely remain on the streets or in unstable and potentially dangerous living situations" (213).

Denise was probably legally eligible for child protective services because of her circumstances. She did not have a viable home. The clause pertaining to "youth who cannot return home" lends itself to interpretation. This screening worker discredited Denise's request for services, claiming that since Denise's mother had a home, Denise could live there. For reasons unidentified and unexplored by the worker, Denise's mother was not providing Denise with any support. When kept out of the system, disenfranchised youth remain invisible and are forced to live precariously. The screening worker did not liberally interpret the law. Restrictive interpretations were common because of limited funds, lack of public will, and punitive youth stereotypes. The language of the law allowed leeway in possible interpretations.

The support Denise required fell most readily under the mandates held by CYS, since she was not eighteen years old. She fell through the cracks of the adult public welfare system. Denise talked about not being able to receive public assistance because of her estranged relationship with her mother. Reform to welfare laws directly affected teen parents through the Personal Responsibility and Work Opportunity Reconciliation Act of 1996 and the creation of the Temporary Assistance to Needy Families (TANF) program. Denise claimed that she could not receive public benefits except through her mother's case. Under the law, to receive TANF benefits, "a teenage mother must either live with his or her parents, a legal guardian, or other adult relative who is at least 18 years old. . . . In these situations, it is the parent . . . or other adult who is the payee on behalf of the minor parent and his or her child" (Juvenile Law Center 2012: 1).

Shifting narratives around individual responsibility, victimization, and youth deviance created a confusing terrain for youth to negotiate. Inconsistent and stigmatized ideas about adolescent mothers reinforced shortsighted policies and interpretations, which hindered their care. The following discussion considers how youth negotiated narratives of independence and redemption not just in the SIL program but also in outside programs. Similar narratives shaped procedures and interactions in a federally funded job-training program.

Producing the Responsible Worker

SIL officials arranged for two representatives from the federally funded program to speak to SIL teen moms at the program's GED classroom. The ceiling was very low and I had to crouch down on a narrow and crooked stairway to enter the basement classroom. It was a cold and snowy day, and Nicole entered with her friend Lisa in a loud, dramatic manner. "Oh, my God!" she exclaimed. "I can't believe you all made us come out here in the snow."

Ms. Brooks, the representative from the job-training program, was a black woman who appeared to be in her mid-thirties. She arrived with another black career counselor, as a couple of other teen moms from the SIL program took their seats around the table. Ms. Brooks began by asking the girls to introduce themselves and share what they had learned from the SIL program. Nicole started laughing and looked at Lisa, who also began to chuckle. Nicole then muttered an inaudible comment and Lisa did the same. Erica looked as though she was trying very hard not to join in the laughter. She offered that she received daycare, had graduated from high school, and had set her future educational and career goals. Ebony mumbled that she had learned to be responsible with school.

Nicole and Lisa's clowning did not impress Ms. Brooks. She told the four girls that in order to benefit from the education and job-training program, applicants must be "serious." "I am going to be brutally honest," she said gravely. "There are a couple of you here who wouldn't qualify." I heard Lisa, who was sitting next to me, whisper, "Nicole and me." Nicole immediately raised her hand and, after being called on, looked directly at Ms. Brooks and said, "When it comes to school, I am very serious." Ms. Brooks replied, "Well, I started assessing you all from the first moment I walked in. If you want consideration for this program, you need to make a good impression." From that moment on, Nicole remained focused and attentive. She did not laugh or smile. She even seemed to rise out of her slouched posture and sit straighter. Her demeanor was calm and she kept her attention directly on Ms. Brooks.

When Nicole entered the room, she conformed her behavior to the social incentives she read from her peers. She either ignored or misread the signals from Ms. Brooks that she must perform a serious, "school" identity. When Nicole realized the disjuncture in Ms. Brooks's reading, she changed her behavior to conform to her expectations. Her transformation provides another example of how youth were flexible and strategic in managing their identities. It also indicated that she was sufficiently motivated by the incentives Ms. Brooks communicated.

I later learned from the job-training program's website that to qualify, youth (ages sixteen through twenty-four) had to meet a low-income requirement. Youth applicants needed to experience at least one of the following circumstances: having dropped out of school, having become parents, being homeless, or living in foster care. During the meeting, Ms. Brooks corrected the public misconception that the job-training program was an alternative school for "bad kids." She emphasized that the program was selective, suggesting that not everyone would get accepted. Applicants were asked to write a five-year plan and an essay about why they deserved a scholarship, which was worth $31,700 per year. I later learned that the benefits included health care, meals, weekly stipends, and a public transportation pass in addition to education and job training. "If you come in and handle your business," Ms. Brooks said, "the opportunities are endless. There is a lot of love in the program and we will bend over backwards for you."

Ms. Brooks claimed that the program supported successful graduates in college, and she repeatedly emphasized the importance of being serious, attending school regularly, and staying away from fights, drugs, or any other signs of disruptive behavior. At one point, Erica interrupted and explained that since she and the other girls had kids, they were motivated to do well and complete the program.

Ms. Brooks acknowledged Erica's comment but reiterated that the program cost a lot of money and the government wanted to spend its funds wisely. Ms. Brooks ended by posing the question, "What type of student are we looking for?" Nicole answered immediately, "Me!" Ms. Brooks smiled and replied, "Good answer. Why you?" Nicole exclaimed, "Because I am going to do it!" Ms. Brooks continued to gaze affectionately at Nicole and offered, "I didn't know about you in the beginning but you are starting to redeem yourself. I like the way you are coming around." Ms. Brooks rewarded Nicole with a clock embossed with the name of the program.

In this context, the administrator used a model of the deserving poor to determine which youth she believed were amenable and worth investment. Worthy youth needed to prove that they were hardworking, focused, and independent. Her presentation included a theme of redemption that was highlighted by Nicole's transformation. Several days later, at the orientation to the federally funded program, this theme of redemption was again evident. The program held the orientation at the job-training site, and approximately 100 applicants attended. They sat in groups of eight or ten at tables in a large cafeteria. The audience consisted mostly of youth of color. The adults present appeared to be parents or family members of the youth applicants. At one point during the session, a young man called out that this program was his very last chance. Staff members and youth alike offered narratives about how the program could change wayward and undisciplined ways. Aimee Cox (2007: 55) explains, "Populations [are] targeted to need improvement, reeducation, and training in order to assimilate into our increasingly privatized, corporate-fed and consumer-driven economy."

The program's website did not report statistics on rates of college attendance among program completers, despite Ms. Brooks's promises of college. The site simply indicated that 77 percent of program graduates entered employment, while 10 percent enrolled in education. It did not indicate which percentage of those entering education enrolled in college. The website also stated that "society" would benefit from "trained entry-level employees." The setting attended by SIL youth provided training in culinary arts, facility maintenance, medical office support, and home health-care and nursing assistance. Thus youth were prepared to join the ranks of the working poor. Program completers reported average wages at $8.03 an hour, despite the program brochure's claim of high-paying jobs.

Programs such as this one for "at risk" youth discursively promoted self-sufficiency and high expectations but did not provide mechanisms to assist youth in achieving these outcomes (Lesko 1995). Lesko suggests, "In not questioning traditional expectations for so-called good mothers within unequal social structures, girls are left with expectations for independence and self-sufficiency but with few public supports or critical understanding of how difficult self-sufficiency is for U.S. single mothers, regardless of age" (199). The federal job-training program did not address the problem of what Lesko (1990, 1995) calls "pink-collar ghetto wages," and it did not prepare girls to make occupational choices outside these low-paying fields. Federal funds prepared girls for a sexist and class-stratified service economy. The job-training program did not prepare them for the better futures they dreamed about.

In *Both Hands Tied*, Jane Collins and Victoria Mayer (2010) depict the changing work demands experienced by adult female welfare recipients. These include the devaluation of unpaid care work, a rhetorical emphasis on autonomy, and the expansion of low-paid service jobs without benefits. Similarly, Frank Ridzi (2009: 10) mentions that "there is little evidence to suggest that the work-first approach does anything more than leave poor parents permanently stranded in the low-wage labor market." Welfare recipients maintain that work-first is "creating a workforce of slave laborers" (3). Poor adolescents and adult women are prepared for the same type of jobs, without avenues for advancement and mobility. Youth in the SIL program were funneled onto the bottom rungs of a service economy, where they would likely remain stuck in poverty for their adult years.

Conclusion

Providers imagined a less than adequate future for young mothers in SIL, despite rhetoric to the contrary. Officials expected youth to become self-controlled and amenable low-skilled workers. Although these views were not completely absent, regulators rarely perceived young mothers as resilient and efficacious. One after-noon, Nel, a caseworker, described her SIL clients. Previously, Nel had worked for several years with incarcerated women in a different state, and her perspective struck me as unusual compared to what I generally heard. Nel spoke about a staff meeting with the SIL di-rector in which Beth asked the workers to raise their hands if they thought the girls had been abused. According to Nel, Beth suggested that 100 percent of the clients had been sexually abused. Nel dis-agreed. She believed that each girl was different and that as a group they had not experienced any one circumstance.

Nel looked at me directly (something she generally avoided) and said matter-of-factly, "Some of them are extremely intelligent." She suggested that a subset of her clients would *choose* the street lifestyle and others would end up in women's prison and do very well there. What does it mean to do well in prison? Nel contested the dominant victim narrative expressed by many, including her supervisor. She cautioned against an overly deterministic understanding of these girls' lives. Was there a touch of irony in Nel's comment? She seemed to imply that society had constructed the cages of street violence and the prison; now it could watch as these resilient young women did quite well in these worlds, perfecting alternate cultural codes. Such a view would seem to normalize punitive forms of contain-ment for this category of marked young women. The standpoints of youth coming of age in inner-city, segregated, impoverished com-munities are influenced through structural injustices. Their choices must be considered in such contexts. Policymakers, service provid-ers, and the public should acknowledge youth resilience and at the same time pay attention to the ways oppressive conditions limit how strengths get expressed. With understanding should come system restructuring. These youth, like all youth, require just options for forming their identities.

This chapter has explored how shortsighted representations of youth contributed to the SIL program's inability to meet its mission of client care. We have also seen the inequitable process through which providers and clients, while positioned distinctly, both re-inforced normative ideologies of individual responsibility and cli-ent spectacles. Focus on individual "problems" and performances preclude attention to the contexts that create problems and make them prevalent. We cannot continue to ask youth to shoulder the burdens of marginalization, which are constructed through our systems of child welfare, education, health care, and employment. Youth are in the process of becoming, and they learn who they are and who they will be through interacting with others. Punitive and shortsighted representations become mirrors in which youth reflect back what they see or contest the images. In the formal service situations described in this chapter, youth experienced high stakes to maintain the impressions of their regulators. However, some mothers engaged in everyday acts of resistance, particularly in program familiar zones. Chapter 2 touched upon these struggles, and we will explore resistance more fully in chapter 5. But next, I provide a detailed case study of one young mother's service negotiations with the Public Housing Authority. Her story provides an opportunity to look in detail at a youth's experiences moving across a number of different service contexts. This portrayal opens a window on how she perceived her own identity performances.

I Am Young. I'm Not Dumb; and I'm Not Anxious

Identity Performances as Service Negotiation

In this chapter, I explore my relationship with one young mother, Nyisha, as I shadowed her across multiple settings and we negotiated services. The different social categories we each occupied framed our strategies, as well as the outcomes. Choices are always made within particular cultural contexts and are constrained or facilitated by the social categories one occupies (Rose 1999; Spencer 2006). Nyisha lived through oppressive conditions for her entire childhood. She was a survivor. For her, the SIL program was a blessing, as she finally had a home of her own making. Her apartment brought her a sense of freedom from the abusive constraints of living in other people's homes. The SIL apartment provided a space in which Nyisha could make some of her own choices. However, her lack of power in the child welfare system constrained her decisions. She needed to rely on inconsistent caseworkers to manage her case. As a white, middle-class, well-educated, adult advocate, I was usually regarded more respectfully by officials or, at the very least, regarded. Because of my position of privilege, I was used to having my views taken seriously.

This case study depicts the effects of cumbersome procedural protocols, spatial barriers, and paradoxes in representation. It provides a closer look at broad themes we have already explored. We see Nyisha's skill in managing the impressions she presented to officials—she knew that she needed to be perceived as deserving. Our interactions with one another suggest the importance of ongoing, supportive relationships between youth and advocates. Positive relationships are essential for successfully negotiating service systems. Structural problems generally compromised these types of relationships between caseworkers and clients in SIL.

Nyisha's Background

For most of Nyisha's life, her mother had been abusing drugs. Her mother was in and out of prison and sometimes homeless. This meant that Nyisha also was often homeless and left to fend for herself. During an interview, she described the hardships involved with not having a place to sleep or food to eat. With too many other pressing concerns, she stopped going to school and would either spend time at a friend's house or shoplift from a corner grocery market in order to get a meal. Even when she attended school, she "hated" it. She recalled,

> Everyone would just pick on me. . . . I never had any friends from school. It was so hard for me. . . . Yeah, so I was just the dirty kid.

She fought back. She was tiny, and the other students teased her because she had to wear the same clothes each day. She shared a story about wearing the same skirt for an entire summer, during which it became too small. At the time she lived at her aunt's house, and her aunt would ask Nyisha to pick out clothes from a catalog—clothes the aunt would order for her own two daughters, neglecting Nyisha.

NYISHA: Yeah, it was just hard. I didn't have nowhere to go. I was fifteen and anyone would just tell me to get out in a heartbeat. You got to go. I don't want you anymore, get out of my house.

LAUREN: That's a tough situation to have to deal with.

NYISHA: That's when I started the [illegal activity].

LAUREN: Because you didn't have anyplace to go?

NYISHA: I had nothing! I had no money to feed myself. I had no money to buy clothes. School was definitely not an option because I couldn't be worried about it. I couldn't even eat. I mean couldn't even get myself something to eat let alone buy books to go to school. . . . Some people would take me up for a little while, treat me like crap. But I don't have nowhere to live, so I would take it. I really didn't have nowhere to go.

At fifteen, Nyisha went to work for an older brother's wife, whom she had looked up to as a role model. Nyisha was manipulated into illegal activity and was caught, locked up for a while, and then put on probation. Her probationary status brought her to the attention of CYS. The screening worker considered her eligible for the SIL program. When Nyisha's probation officer discovered that Nyisha was being abused, he set up an interview for her with the SIL program. Nyisha remembered in great detail her interview and the intake worker's compassion for her situation. Her face brightened into a wide smile as she relayed her feelings:

> This program has to be the best thing that ever happened to me. I can honestly say if I wasn't in this program I would either be in jail or found somewhere dead.

Other young mothers made similar statements during interviews. The SIL program removes youth from extremely detrimental situations and provides them with a residence. It is essential that we maintain and improve these programs to provide for the comprehensive care of young moms, such as Nyisha, and their children.

I had known Nyisha for three years. I met her in 2001 when she was seventeen years old and I was a SIL program manager. I counseled Nyisha after she was gang-raped. Unwilling to speak to a therapist, she agreed to talk with me about her feelings. Over several months, I would take Nyisha to lunch, to pick up job applications, and to visit a local university campus. On only one occasion did she share with me the details of the rape. She said she mostly coped by trying not to think about it. We spent most of our time together talking about other things in her life, such as her experiences in an alternative high school evening program and her hopes to attend college.

This brief discussion of Nyisha's background illustrates her remarkable resilience in spite of abuse and trauma. Nyisha and I had a strong foundation based on the years we had known each other and the trust that we had developed. On several occasions, I referred to Nyisha affectionately as the "Energizer bunny." I remember the first time I used this term, she responded with laughter. I exclaimed how, as with the Energizer bunny, nothing seemed to knock her down. No matter how difficult or frustrating the situation, Nyisha would keep going. This petite young African American mom had been through enormous trials and had suffered abuse and victimization beyond what I've described here. Yet my conviction was repeatedly reaffirmed by her positive attitude, the luminous smile on her face, and her tremendous source of energy, which rarely seemed depleted.

Nyisha's circumstances show how a youth can be pushed into delinquency when she has no other viable means of survival. Through Nyisha's story, we can understand better how school becomes a low priority for youth who have to worry about survival first. Nyisha's experiences were not unique to her. I heard similar themes of poverty, homelessness, abuse, neglect, delinquency, and school hardship in many of the young mothers' stories. Youth shared common struggles negotiating the child welfare system and other public systems.

In 2004, when I began the research for this project, Nyisha and I quickly reestablished our rapport. I learned about the trouble she was having around securing housing. Nyisha worked a variety of retail jobs that paid too little for her to support herself and her three-year-old son, Malcolm, without public assistance. Nyisha was on a board extension with the child welfare system and was quickly approaching her twenty-first birthday. On her birthday, the system would discharge her because of her age and she would no longer be eligible to receive SIL services. This change in status meant that she would need to secure housing, health care, and sufficient resources to support Malcolm and herself. Nyisha hoped to receive publicly subsidized housing. She followed the appropriate steps, filling out many forms, providing multiple means of identity verification, and participating in a housing interview.

One of the greatest challenges faced by youth who age out of the child welfare system is finding affordable housing. It is a key impediment to successful transitions. The majority of mothers who age out of the SIL program are not financially or socially prepared to live autonomously with their children. Many young mothers face significant educational, mental health, or physical health challenges. Their job prospects tend to include unreliable, low-wage, transient labor in fast food, retail, or low-skilled nursing. These employment options do not generally provide a living wage or health insurance. Youth face precarious living conditions, which are made all the more troublesome by their responsibility for the well-being of their children.

Alisa Field (2004: 229) asserts, "The lack of affordable housing is a problem faced by adults of all ages as well as aging-out youth. However, aging-out youth often feel the lack more acutely because they lack family support and resources." Youth leaving care are particularly at risk for long-term homelessness (Smith 2011). There is a significant shortage of affordable housing in the urban area where this study took place. This drawback reflects a national crisis that has historical roots in the urban renewal projects of the 1940s and 1950s. Urban renewal displaced many low-income, mostly black families who resided in the center city. Families were pushed out of their residences to make room for revenue-building projects, including freeways and downtown redevelopment (Mohl 1993). Public housing is touted as the government's compensation to these families. Yet the government never fully implemented public housing policy, so that "although 15 million households qualify for housing assistance, only about a third of them receive it" (Katz 2001: 121). As Michael Katz indicates, "Unlike AFDC, food stamps, or Supplemental Security Income, housing never became an entitlement" (120–21).

The Undeserving Client?

In early July 2004 Nyisha informed me that the Public Housing Authority (PHA) had denied her housing. Her denial was erroneous and could be attributed to the housing agency's error. I audio-recorded our conversation, which occurred in Nyisha's SIL apartment and lasted for three hours. Malcolm, her son, played and occasionally distracted us with various demands on our attention. At the time, Nyisha did not have a case manager. Alise, her prior worker, had recently left the agency.

NYISHA:When I was there at the [housing] interview, [the worker said,] "You have a balance of $1,200." "Excuse me," [Nyisha responded]. "You have a balance from 1993." I said, "I was born in 1983, and in 1993 I was ten."

LAUREN: DID you say, "That's my mother?"

NYISHA: YES, I told them, "That's my mom." "Well, it's coming up under your name. . . ."

LAUREN: WELL then . . . it's a problem that they need to correct. It's not your fault.

NYISHA: IT'S not, but they seem [to think] like it's the biggest problem in the world.

LAUREN: RIGHT, well, you know how . . . This is what you do; you have to have an advocate with you.

NYISHA: THEY won't listen to me.

LAUREN: LIKE you said, you're young and they're not listening to you, which is a problem. It's not right and it shouldn't happen, but it does.

NYISHA: LIKE Alise kept telling me to call, call, call. I said, "Alise, I've been calling. They always get ignorant with me. . . ." Then I told her [referring to the PHA worker] my situation. She said, "Hold on" and put me on hold for forty-five minutes. She thought I was going to hang up and I never hung up. She said, "Oh, I apologize, I forgot you were on hold." How professional is that? You forgot I was on hold. I'm thinking in my head, "Whatever, you were hoping I would hang up." So she put my name in the computer and the same thing came up. "You owe a balance." I said, "No, that was the problem in the first place, I don't owe a balance. It's my mother." [The PHA worker said,] "I can't do anything about that. This is who you need to call," [which she said] with an attitude.

LAUREN: SO you called that other person and then what happened?

NYISHA: With an attitude, "I can't do nothing about that, so I don't know why she gave you my number." I had Alise call. I mean they gave her as much cooperation as possible. That's wrong. I mean, I am young. I'm not dumb; and I'm not anxious. Because if I was anxious, I had my [housing] interview in January, I'd have been on your heels back then. I mean this is like what I need. . . . I'm not saying like, "OK, where's my money? I need my money so I can go clothes shopping." This is serious.

Nyisha tried to contest a dominant representation of the unde-serving, poor young black mother. She perceived this prejudgment from the PHA workers. Nyisha positioned herself in relation to two identity categories: the "kind of person" (Gee 2000: 99) who deserves public housing and the kind who does not. Nyisha made an identity "bid" with me as she presented herself as the "kind of person" who was "worth" assistance. She also defined housing as an essential or "serious" need. However, as Katz (2001) notes, the state does not con-sider housing to be a public entitlement. Nyisha felt an obligation to justify her need for public housing and her worth as a responsible, reasonable, and rational individual. She implied an identity that was distinctly visible through class, race, age, and gendered terms.

Later during our conversation, she stated explicitly that her race was an issue:

> I was like, I don't want to be one of those welfare moms, I don't want to be a part of the statistics. . . . It's already bad enough I'm African American.

Nyisha sought to separate her identity from the welfare mom stereo-type (Strauss and Quinn 1997). When she said it was "bad enough" being African American, she implied that her racial identity alone made her susceptible to stigma, discrimination, and low social sta-tus. Critical race theorists acknowledge the pain and frustration that people of color experience as they negotiate dichotomous good and bad black identities. Anthony Farley (2002: 140) posits that both roles are "identity traps" because they reinforce the rules of inequal-ity structures.

In the roles of both researcher and advocate, I volunteered to accompany Nyisha to the local PHA office. Nyisha knew that I was researching her service negotiations and that I planned to write a book. Soon after our experiences with the PHA, I asked whether I could use this material for an entire chapter and she agreed. I be-lieve that she perceived me first and foremost as her advocate and mentor. Because of my prior position, I knew that she needed an adult advocate for PHA workers to take her request seriously. Both Nyisha and I knew the rules of the system and were unhappy with the ways officials disempowered her.

I learned from another SIL caseworker that Nyisha's mother had used Nyisha's Social Security number to get PHA housing many years prior to our encounter. This fact complicated our ability to improve Nyisha's situation. Nyisha never expressed frustration with her mother for using her Social Security number, ruining her credit, and compromising her ability to receive assistance. Several days later when I picked up Nyisha to take her to the PHA, she mentioned that Malcolm was going with us. He couldn't stay with her mom because her mom had to travel to meet with her probation officer. Nyisha's mother was living in Nyisha's SIL apartment (against SIL rules) and appeared to be dependent on Nyisha for support. As we left the SIL apartment, her mom asked her for money to take the subway and buy an ice cream. Nyisha gave her mom a token and admonished her for the ice cream request. She said she did not have the extra cash for sweets.

Producing Identities in Conflict

As we walked into the PHA, we noticed two service areas on either side of the room, with a glasslike partition separating the work areas from the public. Across from the partitioned zones, people sat in chairs waiting. A stairway between the service areas wound to upper-level offices. Nyisha, Malcolm, and I stood fixed, looking at two booths along opposite walls. I randomly moved toward the booth with no line. Immediately, someone directed us to the other one, where a line had already formed. The partition tended to be a replicable fixture across sites, creating a boundary between public workers and clients. It muffled voices and thus compromised clear communication. The partition did not appear to serve any function other than to establish a distinction between worker and client.

I had noticed that a similar partition separated the front desk from the waiting area in the main CYS building. This high-rise, located downtown, had two entrances, one for the CYS workers and one for the families. Only the front desk at the families' entrance was partitioned. The workers' entrance was not encased. Before reaching the desk on the family side, all clients had to pass through a metal detector. I observed similar partitions at Chinese stores and corner markets in predominately low-income African American neighborhoods. In addition to delimiting those who provided the services from those who received them, the physical boundary of a partition also served to marginalize clients.

As we waited, I held Malcolm's hand. Another woman in line asked whether he was my son. I replied, "No, he is her son," pointing to Nyisha. Nyisha and I looked at each other and giggled quietly. Nyisha whispered to me, "Your boyfriend must be very dark!"

Another woman then stepped in front of us in line. Before we had time to respond, she began to talk to the worker behind a small window. Nyisha and I glanced at each other in annoyance and moved closer together. Immediately before Nyisha's turn, she whispered to me, "You talk." I replied calmly, "No, it's OK. You can talk." I was aware of the power dynamic and wanted her to know that I believed she could communicate effectively.

The female PHA worker opened the window in the partition and Nyisha explained that she had applied for housing but was denied because of a bill her mother owed. The official's gaze remained fixed on her computer screen, and she did not directly acknowledge Nyisha. She asked for Nyisha's Social Security number, typing it into the computer. The worker stated that her records indicated that Nyisha owed $1,200 to the PHA. Nyisha responded calmly that she did not owe the PHA and she was ten years old at the time the debt was accrued by her mother. The worker said that Nyisha should have received a letter, which explained the protocol. If Nyisha wanted to contest the denial, she would need to apply for a hearing. Nyisha replied that she had not received a letter and the worker asked brusquely, how then she had learned about the denial. Nyisha explained that she lives in a SIL program building and the agency had been talking to the PHA on her behalf. The program probably received the letter about the need for a hearing, Nyisha continued, without her knowledge.

I asked the worker behind the partition whether we could talk to a supervisor. I was aware of the long line of women behind us and the public display that was created as we conversed. The worker seemed disinterested in helping Nyisha. I knew that if we were to have any chance of getting the denial reversed quickly, we would need to "justify" the request. I did not want Nyisha's vulnerabilities exposed to a crowd of onlookers. The worker responded that she was the supervisor and she refused my request. I pleaded with her, emphasizing the time-sensitive nature of this issue and that we simply wanted to discuss other options. The expressions on both Nyisha's face and my own must have been particularly desperate because the woman hesitatingly agreed to our request. She told us that we would need to wait. We later learned that it was unorthodox for the supervisor to attend the front desk. Her presence was necessary on this particular morning because her entire staff was attending a training session. She usually worked from her administrative office, located in a private area of the building.

The prior phone conversations with PHA workers were not documented and, therefore, did not exist in the public record. James Scott (1998) contends that it is through administrative processes, including record keeping, that officials are able to maintain power. These acts produce a form of official knowledge that tends to ignore messy aspects of service provision. All of Nyisha's previous attempts to get the records corrected were invisible and, thus, futile. The only records that had been kept referred to the PHA's actions, which encompassed the letter regarding Nyisha's housing denial and communication about the hearing requirement. PHA documentation placed the institution in a position of power, while the absence of records constructed Nyisha's personal agency as inconsequential.

Several weeks prior, Nyisha had described the interpersonal dynamics of her phone conversations. Officials used curt tones to address her, and she believed that officials perceived her as "dumb." She bemoaned her lack of power in negotiations. Lack of personal power also resulted from relying on SIL workers who did not always complete their responsibilities. The scene at the partition repeated these challenges.

The Border Zone

Cheryl Mattingly's (2008) concept of the "border zone" helps inform an understanding of identity negotiations in this service context. Mattingly suggests that a cultural border zone develops when individuals draw on narratives at odds with one another. A worker may not favorably interpret the client's bid for identity recognition. At the border, encounters between clients and officials reinforce cultural differences and identity stereotypes. According to Mattingly, border zones are constructed through two social processes: narrating with conflicting story lines and stereotyping. Identity stereotypes are cultural models, or shared schema, for understanding particular "kinds" of people (Strauss and Quinn 1997). Individuals reinforce stereotypes (at the border) when they assimilate new interactions through already established cultural models. These borders are not inflexible. Sometimes experiences motivate individuals to negate preexisting stereotypes (Strauss and Quinn 1997).

In the PHA front office, Nyisha and the PHA worker constructed a border zone through ritualized interactions. While the inconsistencies in story lines used by Nyisha and the worker constructed the border, physical boundaries and structural inconsistencies reinforced it. The physical partition muffled communication and hindered connection. A long line of women waiting behind us blocked sustained attention from the worker. These physical circumstances reinforced stereotyped constructions from each of us. In chapter 3, I described how I served as an intermediary and reinforced the border zone between the CYS screening worker and Denise. The PHA worker's story line indicated that Nyisha was just another client who had not followed the official protocol: Nyisha had failed to apply for a hearing. Nyisha and I constructed the worker as just another uncaring and rude official. Nyisha made a bid to be recognized as a respectful client, one who intended to follow protocol but had been prevented from doing so by circumstances outside her control: SIL staff had not notified her about the need for a hearing.

Requesting a hearing would have been infeasible because the SIL program planned to discharge Nyisha in two days. Again, Nyisha emphasized the PHA's mistake, which caused her housing denial. In Nyisha's and my own story lines, an official could easily correct the mistake in the record. The mistake, whatever its nature, was inconsequential to the worker. According to her, the official protocol was the only way to contest a PHA decision legitimately. Structural barriers reinforced the disconnected story lines.

The physical boundary presented by the partition signified the emotional and social boundaries upheld by officials and clients. Because housing needs in the city far exceeded public housing resources, officials denied many requests. A partition was functional for the system's officials. Every day PHA workers would come face to face with many individuals to whom they could not provide assistance. Compassion would be overwhelming for these workers. Even after the PHA accepted individuals' applications, women could remain on a waiting list for years before receiving a residence.[1]

The housing protocol included a sequence of narrowly defined tasks that applicants had to follow in the proper order. These procedures maintained the legitimacy of the PHA but did not account for unique personal circumstances and organizational barriers. As bureaucratic tools, protocols differentiated who would get services. These tools enabled public gatekeepers to justify the rationing of resources. Rigid protocols also restricted access to childcare and health care for young families. In chapter 2, I described the cumbersome childcare protocol; I will discuss a health-care protocol in chapter 5. Protocols and documentation processes inhibited the capacity of service systems to respond to complexities in clients' lived experiences (Prussing 2008).

While we waited for the supervisor to return to meet with us, Nyisha and I quietly shared our frustrations. Both of us were dismayed because we believed that the supervisor had discounted Nyisha's situation. Attributes essential to successful service negotiation include persistence, as well as an ability to censor oneself and not react harshly to disrespectful treatment. Both of us were cognizant of the need to perform particular types of identities. Nyisha tried to appear as a self-controlled, respectful client, in spite of her annoyance with the worker. As a white, middle-class, adult advocate, I embodied privileges and expected that officials would address my concerns. In fact, Nyisha said she was glad I had pushed the supervisor for a meeting in her office. It wouldn't have occurred to her that she had the right to request more attention. Other clients made similar observations following joint negotiations in different service contexts. I did not have the stigma of *welfare mother* weighing on my shoulders and thus felt free to advocate. I encouraged the girls, suggesting that they too could use persistence as a strategy. As an advocate, I did not provide anything extraordinary. The conditions I worked under were different from the challenges faced by many case managers. I had the time to invest in Nyisha and other young families.

Changing the Story Line

Surprisingly, we did not wait long for the supervisor to escort us to her back office. As we walked down the winding hallway, I thanked the supervisor for meeting with us, thanks she curtly acknowledged. In the office, Malcolm sat on my lap and Nyisha sat next to me. The three of us were on the same side of a table facing the supervisor. Nyisha again explained her situation and her imminent discharge from the SIL program. The supervisor flipped through a paper copy of Nyisha's PHA file. Her affect began to change. Here in her office, she started to treat us respectfully, her communication style shifting almost instantaneously. "I'm sorry I never introduced myself," she said, extending her hand to us. "I'm Rachel Coleman."

Ms. Coleman's tone of voice elevated, the expression on her face turned pleasant, and she began looking us in the eye. Ms. Coleman was African American and apparently in her mid-thirties. She was dressed professionally in a dark pantsuit, and her hair was cropped close to her head. Ms. Coleman called an upper-level administrator at another location and spoke to her loudly in an animated tone. The abrupt, matter-of-fact worker who had addressed us at the partitioned front desk had transformed into a cooperative, excitable woman in this private, more welcoming office. The phone conversation was on speaker as our new supporter explained Nyisha's situation to the female administrator. She asked whether there was anything that could be done immediately to appeal the denial and assign housing. The administrator on the other end of the phone asked who the site manager was and Ms. Coleman responded exuberantly, "Me!" She seemed excited to share this information, and I inferred that she must have moved up through the ranks of PHA. The administrator chuckled at Ms. Coleman's tone and explained that Ms. Coleman had the authority to override the housing denial without a hearing. When Nyisha and I heard this, I squeezed her knee and we looked at each other with huge smiles. Ms. Coleman immediately pulled up her housing database and started searching for a residence for Nyisha and Malcolm. Nyisha exclaimed, "Oh, my God, I can't believe this! I was so stressed." She covered her mouth and began to cry. I looked at Nyisha and also started to tear up as Ms. Coleman said, "You two better stop it or you'll make me cry."

Ms. Coleman also took an interest in keeping Malcolm entertained and content. She provided him with a large box of toys. Malcolm situated himself on the floor and proceeded to unload the entire box. Nyisha admonished Malcolm for making such a mess, but Ms. Coleman did not seem the least bit annoyed. She said Malcolm was welcome to play with as many toys as he wanted. She even gave him a package of crackers and seemed not to notice as he scattered crumbs on the floor around him. Ms. Coleman explained with a grin that she had a five-year-old son, so she was familiar with little-boy antics. Maybe Ms. Coleman saw parts of herself in Nyisha, perhaps reminding her of her own trials as a black mother of a young boy. This connection could be supported only in an environment free from the normative boundary signifiers that separated clients and public officials. Regardless of Ms. Coleman's personal feelings toward Nyisha and her son, her ability to override the protocol demonstrated the protocol's socially constructed nature.

This vignette shows how a sociospatial setting can support the restructuring of guiding narratives and communication patterns between public officials and clients. However, these contexts were not deterministic (Duranti 1994; Goodwin and Duranti 1992). Ms. Coleman's personal agency and organizational position were essential, as it was her prerogative to meet with us in her private office. It was also her decision to override the hearing and to grant Nyisha immediate housing. Nyisha and I were able to effect Ms. Coleman's decision only indirectly.

The protocol created an illusion of an intractable and "encompassing" system (Ferguson and Gupta 2002: 981). However, the rigid protocol was actually bending: Ms. Coleman was able to swiftly override it. The border zone resulted not from an inability to understand one another but, rather, from structural and physical occlusion (i.e., through the protocol and the partition). In the front office space, Ms. Coleman tried to protect the legitimacy of the PHA agency by appearing not to favor Nyisha over other applicants. She was under the surveillance of other officials and the broader public. Once these situational and physical boundaries were removed, we all engaged more freely. We were able to communicate different aspects of our identities. Nyisha and Ms. Coleman connected across the border.

Ms. Coleman created a relaxed, more intimate climate in the private office. In fact, Ms. Coleman and Nyisha reflected freely on their performances earlier that morning. Ms. Coleman joked that she had almost had to throw Nyisha out because she was hollering so loudly. Nyisha responded, "Oh, no, I was trying to use big words and I wanted to be really polite but I was so nervous!" Ms. Coleman looked at Nyisha with a grin that appeared friendly. She exclaimed, "You know I'm just joking with you." Nyisha continued, "I know you deal with a lot of 'ignorant people' and I was trying really hard not to be one of them. But I know the words just didn't come out right." Ms. Coleman said Nyisha had done a fine job. By stressing this in a joking way, she affirmed Nyisha's worthiness, as well as her own power to accept Nyisha's plea.

Both Ms. Coleman and Nyisha invoked the cultural model of the "ignorant" welfare mother. Nyisha worked her identity (Carbado 2002) to repudiate any association with the stereotype, the same image she had been at pains to disavow several days earlier during our interview. Valerie Walkerdine (2006) argues that "the guarding against the Other position is painful and frightening" (18) and there is no place for mistakes. An ethos of fear informed these identity struggles because Nyisha could become homeless if identified as an undeserving applicant. The open dialogue was safely embraced only through continued efforts to demarcate social status differences. Within this intimate space, Ms. Coleman evaluated Nyisha as the "kind of person" (Gee 2000: 99) who deserved public assistance. Nyisha could be a deserving client only in contrast to the undeserving, "ignorant" client. The stereotyped cultural model was preserved.

Even as the border zone was socially constructed, it was not easily transgressed. It was repeatedly enacted through cultural scripts of what it meant to be a client and what it meant to be an official. Physical boundaries and cumbersome procedures reinforced the border. It took several unusual and unpredictable circumstances for us to receive a private meeting. The housing protocol caused setbacks for the many families who were unable to follow it successfully.

Frustrated Fulfillment

Ms. Coleman directed us to another PHA administrator's private office. Mr. Allen, a white administrator for the PHA, finalized the housing assignment. He gave Nyisha an official form and told her not to lose this paper, as it was "gold." He said the housing included a community center with computers. As we were leaving the PHA, Nyisha confided that she had been up nights crying in her bathroom because she didn't want Malcolm to hear her. She had no idea what she was going to do about housing, and now she felt such a sense of relief that she wanted to scream. In silence and anticipation, we walked two blocks. I looked at this small-framed young woman as her relief erupted physically. She balled her fists and let out a piercing scream, which disrupted the street-side complacency.

A few days later, I went with Nyisha and Malcolm to preview their assigned PHA apartment and we chatted comfortably in my car. The SIL program provided Nyisha with a few extra days in her residence until she would be able to move into the PHA apartment. She was in good spirits and talked excitedly. She gave me samples of lotions from her new job as a sales clerk at a local department store. She also showed me the form from the public health clinic, which documented her receipt of required immunizations to get back in school. She planned to reenroll in the high school evening program that same day, after her housing appointment. I was truly proud of her and congratulated her on the ways she was moving forward in all areas of her life. A positive outcome in Nyisha's life—receiving public housing—had helped her feel more motivated overall about her circumstances. Although she was unenthusiastic about returning to high school, she was excited about the prospect of starting college. Her sense of hope offset the challenges she would face in what she perceived as a punitive and infantilizing high school environment. She was taking the steps needed to move toward her multiple goals.[2]

After arriving at the PHA site, we waited briefly for the maintenance man, who was to show us the apartment. He was a fairly heavy-set, middle-aged African American man with a pleasant grin and a kind expression. Nyisha and I each took one of Malcolm's hands as we followed the man across the courtyard. Malcolm started jumping around and talking excitedly, and Nyisha sternly mumbled under her breath for him to settle down. I felt conscious of the many eyes on us. A group of about twelve young men stood close to the entrance of the high-rise. The floor in the front entrance was covered in cardboard, and the smell reminded me of the unpleasant scent in my college dormitory many years earlier. We took the elevator to the eighth floor. As we walked out of the elevator, I noticed a wall with colored cement blocks where a window might be expected. As we approached Nyisha's assigned apartment, I observed that the door handle to the unit was missing.

The apartment was industrial in style, with limited lighting, which created a gray, foreboding atmosphere. The floor was composed of cold white cement, and the walls were built of cinder blocks. A tall fence encompassed the entire outside balcony, and very little natural light entered the apartment. The kitchen appliances looked old, and the cabinets were uneven. The exhaust above the stove was missing, and wires stuck out from the ceiling. We looked at the bathroom; the sink was covered with brown stains, which Nyisha later described as cigarette burns. The maintenance man waited in the main room as the three of us entered one of the two bedrooms. Nyisha muttered, "Oh, my God, I can't live here!" She took my hand and asked, "Lauren, do you see this place?"

I was aware of Nyisha's extreme discomfort. I felt apprehensive because of the limited probability of getting this assignment altered. We would be pressing our luck by going against protocol a second time. Nyisha's apprehension was in stark contrast to her original feelings of joy. Ms. Coleman and Mr. Allen's descriptions had led us to imagine a very different home from what lay before us. Like the partitioned entrance at the public housing office, the construction of this facility communicated distrust and distain for the poor. As we left the apartment, the maintenance man said to Nyisha, "Wherever you end up, I hope you're happy." We waited quietly for the elevator, until a woman's scream in an apartment somewhere along the corridor broke the silence. Nyisha looked at me with widened eyes. As we walked out of the building with a small group of residents, I spotted a roach on the front door. Malcolm screamed, "Roach!" Nyisha appeared embarrassed and admonished him, "Malcolm, be quiet!"

Nyisha gazed at me and said, "I don't want to live here." I suggested that we try to get the assignment changed, even though I knew this would be unlikely. We decided to return to the PHA immediately. It began to rain violently as we drove away, creating an ominous atmosphere that reflected our mood, despite my attempts to appear upbeat. Nyisha feared that Ms. Coleman would reject her request, perceiving her as being "choosy." She uttered barely audibly, "Did you see all those guys? And you know, after what happened to me, I just feel really scared."[3] She said that she would be afraid to enter the building after dark and would be petrified to live there alone with Malcolm.

I suggested that she honestly communicate her experience of the rape and her apprehension about living in a high-rise. I knew she would need to *justify* her request to the PHA administrators. Her face went blank and stoic, and she stared straight ahead for the duration of the car ride. It appeared as though she had resigned herself to the situation. She probably believed that she would end up living in a place where she felt unsafe. Throughout her childhood, Nyisha had been victimized and trapped. She had experienced little control.

When we reached the PHA office, we were turned away abruptly after being informed that Ms. Coleman and Mr. Allen were unavailable. In the car ride back to her SIL apartment, we jointly developed a negotiation strategy for the next day. I was leaving town and would be unable to accompany Nyisha. She was nervous about going alone, but after I offered some encouragement and we deliberated, she felt more comfortable implementing our plan. Acting on her own, Nyisha succeeded in getting her housing assignment changed.

Perseverance: Continued

When I returned to town, I visited Nyisha in her new home. It was located on a narrow block of row houses in a predominately low-income, African American neighborhood—"the ghetto," as Nyisha referred to it. As I walked up the front steps, I noticed her windows did not have curtains and her address was hand-painted on a low section of the porch. A group of men in black suits stood in front of one of the nearby houses. Later, Nyisha explained that they were gathering after a funeral. When I rang the doorbell a young woman I didn't recognize answered the door. Nyisha pushed herself in front of the woman and looked at me with a beaming smile. "Hi, Lauren, come in!" She directed me into her kitchen to view the items she had purchased earlier that day. I noticed that the living room was not yet furnished.

I said to the young woman who had greeted me, "I don't believe we've met." Nyisha replied, "This is my brother's girlfriend." I asked, "Hi, brother's girlfriend, what's your name?" We all chuckled, and she responded that her name was Jackie. She introduced her children to me, a girl, who was seven at the time, and a boy, who was four. I sat at Nyisha's kitchen table while Nyisha ran around pointing out all her purchases. She asked, "Aren't these cute?" as she opened a drawer filled with cutlery with frosted plastic handles. She opened her cupboard and pointed out the glasses and dishware. Then she showed me two lamps and pulled out a box of tea candles. She asked, "Don't these candles smell good?" I matched her excited tone as I praised her new household items. I noticed that while the kitchen was not large, it was renovated with new appliances. This kitchen was a lovely contrast to the one at the PHA high-rise. The bright green counter complemented the freshly painted light-tan walls.

Nyisha exclaimed, "Come on, I want to show you the rest of the house." After she escorted me upstairs, I greeted her mother and Malcolm and we settled in Nyisha's bedroom. Nyisha's room had large bay windows that provided an abundance of light. A pile of clothes was lying in the middle of the floor, and Malcolm and his cousins began jumping around in them. Nyisha yelled for them to stop. I asked whether the clothes were clean, to which she replied yes, with a sheepish grin. I returned her smile and said, "Well, at least they *were* clean." Nyisha moved all the clothes into a laundry bag and sat next to them on the floor. I faced her as I sat on her bed next to Jackie and Nyisha's mother. The kids continued to jump, on and off the bed. There was a lot of commotion; a television was playing loudly in the background, and the kids were screaming and running around playing. At one point, the boys started to fight over a truck of Malcolm's. During all this activity, Nyisha narrated the events that had enabled her to acquire the PHA house.

To inform Jackie, Nyisha and I first told her about the original visits to PHA and the high-rise. Jackie exclaimed that she also needed to get a PHA house. She and her children were living with Jackie's mother, whose place was now crowded. Nyisha told Jackie to visit PHA and make "face to face" contact, because that was the only way to get anything accomplished. Her multiple phone calls produced no result. Nyisha incorporated strategies learned during our service navigation and provided these as advice to Jackie.

Then I asked Nyisha to tell us about how she had acquired this stand-alone home. Nyisha's voice became louder and higher pitched as she narrated the events. Her facial expressions were bold and exaggerated, which added vigor to her story. Nyisha mentioned her newly assigned case manager, Rebecca, from whom she had sought assistance because I was unable to accompany her. The following excerpts are paraphrased from my field notes; I did not audio record.

I went down there to the PHA office really early. Oh no, first I was waiting [at the SIL apartment] for my case manager, Rebecca, and she stood me up. I didn't get down there until late because I had to take the bus. When I looked in, there was a room full of people. So I went outside to use the pay phone and I called Mr. Allen for an appointment. He set it up for 11:30. So I just waited in there. Rebecca finally showed up. [Nyisha mentions Rebecca using an annoyed tone of voice.] Rebecca kept saying they probably wouldn't change the site, but maybe they would put me on a list for an early transfer. Rebecca was being really negative, and she didn't even know what she was talking about. I was thinking, "Well it doesn't hurt to ask." She made me feel really scared, but I kept remembering Lauren saying, "You can do it!" [Nyisha changes her voice to imitate mine, and I laugh at her characterization of me.]

I had provided Nyisha with the phone numbers for both Mr. Allen and Ms. Coleman before leaving town. She resourcefully adjusted the plan we had set when her case manager's negligence forced her to arrive late.[4] Given the conflict-ridden cultural scripts that commonly guide interactions between officials and clients, Nyisha's apprehension was understandable. Furthermore, she had a lot at stake in the outcome of the negotiation. Despite what she described as her case manager's negativity, our prior experiences as a duo and our reflections on these service strategies apparently enabled Nyisha to enact a narrative of empowerment. She incorporated lessons learned into her own approach.

Nyisha assumed responsibility for getting her needs acknowledged and understood that the PHA organization could be pressed to bend. She demonstrated both persistence and flexibility in adapting her plan and pushing the administrators to consider her needs. When shadowing clients, I found that persistence was key to successful negotiations and essential in resisting bureaucratic protocols.

Victimization Narrative: Performing "the Other" Identity

Nyisha continued to describe and enact the meeting with Mr. Allen:

When Mr. Allen called me back, Rebecca wasn't even there. She had left to go get a sandwich. I went in there and told him I didn't feel comfortable at the PHA high-rise. He was sitting back and looking at me with an attitude, like "OK and what do you want me to do?" He said, "Well there's nothing I can do." Then, I got all nervous looking and I even started rubbing my jeans with my hands. [Nyisha imitated this rubbing motion for us.] I said, "Well, ever since I was raped I don't feel comfortable around a bunch of black guys." [Nyisha paused, looked at us, and started laughing loudly. The others smiled at her dramatic performance.] He got all uncomfortable and started looking at his computer to find another house for me. I was like, "Thank you, I was just scared that I would get killed or raped having to go in there." He was thinking like, "Oh, don't say that word again, black girl." But then Rebecca walked in and her sandwich was already half gone. Rebecca asked what was going on, and I motioned he was finding me something. He announced there was a scattered site house, but he had never seen it; so he didn't know what it was like. I said, "Well, it has to better than the high-rise, so I'll take it."

In the privacy of her home, Nyisha reflected on her prior negotiations with Mr. Allen. She presented herself as the astute and powerful victor. She characterized Mr. Allen, the nervous white guy, and Rebecca, the ineffectual sandwich eater, as dupes. This account demonstrates how clients draw on specific narratives to strengthen their positions. Nyisha used the border zone between Mr. Allen and herself to position her request so that he would consider it. At first, he addressed Nyisha with the "attitude" typical of interactions between officials and clients. Nyisha and Mr. Allen began their interaction following divergent story lines: Nyisha wanted her housing assignment changed, and Mr. Allen was not amenable to altering it. Mr. Allen viewed Nyisha through a cultural model of the dependent black welfare mother. Young women in Nyisha's position did not have the right to simply assert preference for alternative residences. As Nikolas Rose (1999) explains, recipients are not considered to be full citizens, and the state does not grant them the privilege to discern. They are rendered as marginal and reliant on the generosity of taxpayers.

Nyisha played the part of a vulnerable victim to highlight her misfortunes and inspire the administrator to act. After she performed a black female victim, a frequently stigmatized but in this case worthy identity, Mr. Allen accommodated her request. Nyisha simultaneously evoked Mr. Allen's cultural models for dangerous black guys and victimized black girls. She transformed a traumatic past experience into a performance of racial spectacle (Farley 2002). Nyisha's trauma story and her emphasis on race elicited Mr. Allen's discomfort. At least this seemed to be Nyisha's perception of the encounter.

Her performance pushed the administrator away from his color-blind, privileged stance (Farley 2002; Valdes, McCristal Culp, and Harris 2002). Nyisha's identity work attended to the race, age, and gender distinctions between Mr. Allen and herself.

While I was not present and did not have the opportunity to speak to Mr. Allen directly, his behavioral shift makes sense in the context of my fieldwork. As I have already noted, decision making among public officials tended to reflect risk management. Once an agency became responsible for a client's welfare, identity politics shifted. For instance, Nyisha asserted her agency as she cleverly reminded Mr. Allen that he was responsible for her safety. Nyisha had already received her "gold" paperwork, which made the PHA responsible for her housing. Public officials risked losing professional status and their jobs if they did not meet the safety expectations set by policy-makers. If Nyisha was "raped" or "killed" at a PHA site, the administrator and his agency would be considered accountable.

Perhaps Mr. Allen made the change because he felt embarrassed and wanted to avoid discussing Nyisha's trauma. He may have felt compassion for her. He may have feared liability. Or he may have experienced a combination of these reactions. Whatever his motivation, Nyisha used the gendered and racial tensions between them to her own advantage. The general culture of fear that dominated public service systems also influenced the outcome. On multiple occasions, SIL officials expressed apprehension about unsafe program environments. They were afraid of being blamed by the state if a client was hurt at their rented properties. These same officials felt powerless because they were unable to stem ongoing violence.

The encounter with Mr. Allen reveals the complex role of the border zone. In the first encounter with Ms. Coleman, we crossed the border when we moved into a more intimate private space. In this familiar zone, Ms. Coleman and Nyisha shared a common story line, and they communicated a fuller spectrum of their identities. The immediate spatial context played a significant role in shifting identities. A sense of intimacy was accessible for Nyisha and Ms. Coleman because they shared race and gender identities and were both mothers of young black boys. Collective histories of oppression create a platform for unification, despite ongoing lived inequalities within racially similar groups (MacKinnon 2002).

Mr. Allen and Nyisha also interacted in a private office, yet border crossing did not occur across both dimensions (story line and identity). Even as Nyisha's performance brought Mr. Allen into agreement with her story line (he assigned her a different house), it made identity stereotypes more rigid. The sociohistorical discursive context (which includes stigmatized cultural models) was more significant than the physical context in shaping identity negotiations. Critical race theories explain mechanisms of intersectionality, in which oppressions along race, gender, class, sexuality, and age dimensions interact in complicated and mutually reinforcing ways (Valdes, McCristal Culp, and Harris 2002). According to Nyisha, she did not connect with Mr. Allen. Ongoing inequality and dissimilarity across multiple identity dimensions made the border between Mr. Allen and Nyisha more difficult to cross. I do not want to suggest that connection between Nyisha and Mr. Allen was impossible, but it would take sustained interactions over time to break out of stereotypical molds.

Conclusion

The victim trope was dominant in public service systems and seemed to precede any individual client who requested assistance. Providers were willing to help someone whose difficulties were not caused by their own actions. Nyisha deliberately disguised her feelings of vulnerability as she played the victim role and enacted a common script. She transformed her suffering from the rape into a performance and a spectacle, which, paradoxically, enabled her to hide and protect her vulnerabilities. Even the audience members in her bedroom did not display any sign of compassion regarding the actual trauma. Instead they smiled at Nyisha's dramatic skit.

Nyisha's identity work suggests W. E. B. Du Bois's concept of "double consciousness." Du Bois (1903) explains the ways blacks view themselves both as objects through the lens of the white observer and as agents through their own self-determined lens (see also Akom 2008). Nyisha could see herself as the black female victim through Mr. Allen's lens, while at the same time she perceived her ability to influence his actions. Du Bois and contemporary critical race theorists emphasize the linguistic, behavioral, and psychological skills (ones clearly evidenced by Nyisha) needed to accomplish identity work in a racially discriminatory society (Akom 2008; Blau and Brown 2001).

Nyisha, Malcolm, and I were active agents. Our trajectory across service contexts was fraught with uncertainty and unpredictability. Nyisha and I applied our knowledge about how to "work the system" as we struggled to overcome bureaucratic structures. We resisted rigid protocols, worked with identity stereotypes, and pushed against spatial confinement. Our negotiations point to the material barriers and limited cultural models that restrict clients' access to publicly provided services. These restrictions are normalized, and barriers are not easily transgressed. It took perseverance, the learning and practice of an empowerment narrative, my availability as an advocate, good luck, and a number of unusual circumstances to overcome the barriers.

"The system" positioned Nyisha in such a way that she had to divulge painful, private memories to a relative stranger in order to justify her request for safe housing. We must remember that many families live in the high-rise that Nyisha, Malcolm, and I visited and other buildings like it. They too probably feel unsafe. Shadowing youth gives us a window into how they perceive their own identity performances. In fact, Sandra Morgen, Joan Acker, and Jill Weigt (2010: 128) note, "When expressions of dissent are muted as a form of self-protection, it may be difficult to discern the potential counter-hegemonic values and beliefs that often survive just below the surface of the culture of compliance." It is important to understand that youth performances do not always reflect internalizations of victim or other punitive identities. Youth are resilient in managing impressions for their regulators. Yet at the same time, we must recognize the injustice of pushing clients, like Nyisha, to mold and "use" personal trauma to justify access to basic necessities.

Michael Nakkula and Eric Toshalis (2008: 12) emphasize how development is constructed through "co-authorship," in which youth and adults together shape each other's life stories. Healthy codevelopment for youth and advocates is undersupported by child welfare structures and cultural conditions. As we have seen, circumstances are deeply intertwined for case managers and clients in the SIL program. In chapter 5, I delve into situations that shaped mothers' daily resistance (oftentimes alongside their caseworkers). In spite of these oppositions, the nature of these resistances did not result in altered structures of governance in child welfare.

The Program Allowed Me to Get Pregnant

Everyday Resistance, Dignity, and Fleeting Collectives

Clients in the SIL program not only managed impressions of themselves by enacting worthiness narratives; in some instances, they also engaged in everyday acts of resistance. I define acts of resistance broadly to include participant tactics that pushed against governance, including opposition to official rules, procedural protocols, and programmatic expectations. Youth expressed opposition individually, in the company of other youth, with caseworkers, or with me as an advocate. Previous chapters have detailed such acts (e.g., Nyisha and I resisting her official housing denial, or case managers and youth resisting a program rule that prohibited male cohabitants). This chapter builds on prior examples and explores more fully how institutional and program contexts shaped resistances. This chapter also looks at the implications of resistant acts. Youth attempted to protect themselves from what they perceived as attacks on their integrity and well-being. Several youth coped by hiding from surveillance and oversight altogether. Rather than resist and face unpredictable consequences, they chose to be silent or invisible. Last, I consider the fleeting formation of youth collectives.

Individual Resistances

Young mothers and their caseworkers commonly engaged in banter, but they were often frustrated with one another. The bantering was in jest and conveyed with a smirk, which seemed to reveal affection between participants. In other instances, arguments revealed underlying animosity and tension. Clients and SIL caseworkers engaged in daily outbursts and minor conflicts. These generally inconsequential disruptions were typical even for participants who had good relationships with one another. Such outbursts were quickly forgotten, and workers rarely punished clients for minor acts of resistance. Caseworkers tended to offer less assistance to mothers with reputations for being rude. But even these youth were not discharged for resistant behavior alone.

Marquitta, a young delinquent mother, offers an example of daily resistance. Governance, bureaucratic obstacles, and lack of comprehensive support shaped her oppositional behavior. Marquitta met the SIL requirement that she attend school. She faced other challenges because of insufficient program support. She was on a board extension with the child welfare system and had two young daughters (ages two years and five months). She planned to graduate from high school just before her twenty-first birthday. CYS did not provide her with childcare services, and her children's father watched the kids in Marquitta's SIL apartment (even though this was against the rules).

I observed a confrontation between Marquitta and her case manager, Rebecca, in the Evergreen office. Marquitta burst into the office and started yelling at Rebecca because Rebecca had disturbed her at school. Rebecca had called with a question that she could have answered easily by looking in Marquitta's file. Marquitta shouted in exasperation at being bothered in the middle of her school day. John, her children's father, entered the office behind her and looked at me with resignation. He did not try to deter Marquitta. Rebecca replied defensively that she had been at the hospital all day with one of her clients. She did not have time to check Marquitta's file. Marquitta retorted sarcastically, "What's that, do you only have one client?" Case managers claimed regularly that they could not focus on any particular client's needs at the expense of the others. They would draw on the "I have many clients" narrative to deflect a particular client's complaint. Marquitta reversed this common narrative to question the worker's devotion to one client at the expense of her own needs.

Marquitta continued in a raised voice, demanding to know how her worker was going to help her and her family. They had six months remaining before Marquitta would age out of the child welfare system. Helen, who was also in the office, asked her whether she had applied for public housing. I did not hear her response but noticed

John tickle the back of her neck, which made her smile. A couple of days later, I met Marquitta at the caseworker's office before a scheduled interview. She had picked up a public housing application from Helen. Marquitta flipped through the many pages and exclaimed that she did not know how she was going to complete it. Not only would she need to complete all the paperwork correctly; she would also need to obtain verifications such as birth certificates for herself and her children, as well as Social Security cards. Because many of the youth in SIL had been homeless, they did not always possess these forms of identification. Obtaining documentation required interactions with several bureaucracies before even beginning the lengthy housing protocol. Marquitta wondered when she would find the time to locate housing. She loved the charter school that she attended and was rarely absent. She felt a sense of accomplishment because she had enrolled at this specialized school after dropping out of school and not attending for years. She worried that the need to prepare her family for transition would compromise her graduation.

During our interview, Marquitta provided the context for her argument with Rebecca. She explained that she had been asking Rebecca for over a month to change her children's doctor. As a youth client, Marquitta depended on her case manager to make such changes. Marquitta was frustrated by multiple unsuccessful attempts to get Rebecca's help. The program manual given to the youth noted that "as you near completion of our program, your case manager will begin working with you around finding your own place to live." Marquitta did not believe that her worker would assist her.

Marquitta tried to plan for her young family's future after the conclusion of SIL program support. Her choice to attend school full time created financial hardship for her family because she no longer worked. Complying with the SIL and CYS mandate to attend school left her and her family vulnerable. Her caseworker was not helping her, and she did not have enough time or resources to locate housing on her own. Furthermore, even if she did pursue housing by herself, outside providers usually ignored or discounted service requests from youth alone. Providers mistrusted and misjudged dependent and delinquent youth, and these perceptions were embedded in system mechanisms. Youth commonly felt overwhelmed by the need to finish school, work, find housing, and provide for their young families. This stress was increased by the difficulty in getting caseworkers to advocate on their behalf. As we have seen, caseworkers faced a number of challenges that compromised their abilities to support clients and complete the many mandated tasks.

Insufficient resources, cumbersome bureaucracies, and inflexible governance created a stressful program context. Conflict was therefore normal between mothers and their caseworkers, particularly in program familiar zones. In these environments, participants found it difficult to sustain trusting and caring relationships. Even clients who appreciated their workers on a personal level would express frustration with the SIL staff's inability to obtain services for them. Higher-level officials were unaware of the interactions between caseworkers and clients in familiar zones. Everyday resistances took place on an interpersonal level that did not result in structural changes or significant shifts in power. Even when organizational and bureaucratic barriers fueled resistance, conflicts happened among individuals who were relatively powerless in the child welfare hierarchy. Clients' (or even case managers') complaints did not change the decisions of power brokers in child welfare.

Addressing the Invisible Higher-Ups

Donique, a seventeen-year-old delinquent mother, resisted outside a familiar zone, in a way unique among the resistances I observed. One afternoon, I visited Donique in her SIL efficiency apartment. After we discussed my research, Donique said she would like to talk to me about living in the SIL program. She began by telling me that she had written a letter and faxed copies of it to all the directors at the Visions agency. In the letter, she expressed her urgent need for daycare because she wanted to attend school. I complimented her on her ability to advocate for herself in such a confident manner. She responded by saying that her caseworkers were reprimanded because they allowed her to use the agency's fax machine to send the letter. I followed her into her kitchen and we continued to talk while she prepared lunch.

Donique was making fried chicken and macaroni and corn, the favorite meal of her son, Samir. She set out packages of frozen macaroni and frozen corn and ran hot water over the frozen chicken to thaw it. I exclaimed how orderly she kept her apartment. She had tidily stacked in her cabinet various cans and boxes of food. She had covered her table with a bright-red cloth, on which she had placed a simple set of salt and pepper shakers. All of Samir's toys were arranged on shelves in the space that in the efficiency functioned as both living room and bedroom. She used her small space well by neatly organizing all her belongings.

Donique exclaimed that her apartment was messy by her standards. Since maintenance men had just sprayed to eliminate roaches, she had moved her bed to the middle of her living room/bedroom. She said the roaches were really bad in this apartment building. At her previous SIL apartment on Willow Avenue, this had not been a problem, but there mice were everywhere. As the hot water continued to run, she declared that she was all ready for school. "Come look at my school stuff." We walked into her living room/bedroom and sat on the couch as she excitedly showed me her new black messenger bag, complete with notebooks and colored highlighters. She was looking forward to starting a GED program at the local community college. Then her voice lowered as she said she probably would not be able to attend because she did not have childcare. I asked whether she knew anyone who could "temporarily" watch Samir, and she said no. She wanted to get back into school because otherwise she would be unable to help Samir with his homework when he started school.

Later that day in the caseworkers' office, Helen and Nel discussed the letter Donique had written. As I did, they perceived it as a positive demonstration of her ability to advocate on her own behalf. They were frustrated by the way administrators had restricted a client's agency and their own practices as advocates. "Don't we live in America and have freedom of speech?" Helen asked rhetorically. She and Nel believed that the administrators' response reflected their tendency to avoid acknowledging dissent. They thought administrators did not want to take responsibility for denied childcare and would rather blame their caseworkers. In fact, administrators often expressed to me their frustrations with their caseworkers, whom they saw as unable to follow protocols.

Administrators blocked a channel of communication with Donique. As we have seen, moms often shared their frustrations about childcare with caseworkers. Donique went outside the normal hierarchy when she communicated her needs directly to the administrators in charge. She pushed them to confront their constructed invisibility. Because upper-level administrators worked from a suburban business office, most of them had never met the clients. Donique communicated that she knew about their existence and their responsibility to provide childcare for her son. She felt entitled to make her request, in spite of limited precedent and the absence of face-to-face encounters with these administrators.[1] Officials ignored Donique's request and did not fix the impossible childcare protocol.

Resistance and Escalation

Because daily resistance tended to take place among players with limited power in program familiar zones, these disruptions did not generally cause great harm. On occasion, however, resistance escalated. The following vignette demonstrates how unstable and unjust governance can influence a client's actions and lead to violence. One morning, I visited the SIL administrative office for a planned interview with Jane, a SIL program manager. I learned from Rose, the administrative assistant, that Jane was at court pressing charges against a client. I waited for about forty-five minutes. Just as I was getting ready to leave, Jane entered the office, apologizing for her lateness and looking a bit frazzled. After we settled in her private office, she told me what had happened to her, repeating the narrative several times over the course of an hour.

She began by showing me where the client had hit her in the face with a cell phone. Although I could not see a mark, I commiserated with her. Jane was clearly upset as she bemoaned the whole situation, which had escalated from an encounter that had gone awry. Repeatedly, she expressed her frustration with the client's CYS worker, who, she claimed, was "stupid" and had instigated the dangerous situation. Jane explained that she had arranged a meeting with the CYS worker, the SIL case manager, and the young mother to make plans for the young woman's discharge from the SIL program.

This client did attend school consistently but regularly smoked marijuana. SIL staff members complained of the "dangerous element" she purportedly brought into the program. SIL workers used the term "dangerous element" as code for male drug dealers. Several days prior to the meeting, Jane said, she had informed the young mom that she would be discharged because of her connection to this "element."

At the meeting with CYS, which took place in the mom's SIL apartment, Jane asked the CYS worker about the plan for the client's next residential placement. Jane suggested that the client should be enrolled in a drug rehabilitation program. The CYS worker responded that the girl would be discharged from CYS because she was eighteen (and on a board extension), at which point child welfare services would cease. However, the worker planned to initiate a "file" on the young mom's son. A file necessitated some degree of CYS oversight but did not require the child's removal from his mother's custody. According to Jane, the girl became extremely upset and started to "cuss and rant." The CYS worker then said to the girl, "Well, if you are going to act like a fool, I am going to take your son away." The CYS worker pulled out her cell phone and arranged to take the boy from his daycare and place him under CYS custody. The young mom was so distraught that she ran out of her SIL apartment. As the officials left the building, the girl approached them from the outside. Jane recounted what followed with a wide-eyed expression. "The client goes crazy and starts kicking the workers' cars." Then she approached the officials and hit Jane in the face with her phone. Another client from the SIL program witnessed this and restrained the girl. The other mom, according to Jane, exclaimed to the girl, "Oh, my God, what have you done?" and tried to justify the distraught mother's behavior.

Jane was irate with the CYS worker, who had disregarded the appropriate protocol for removing a child from a parent's custody. According to Jane, the worker punished the mom for "cussing and ranting" and did not evaluate any evidence about the mom's parenting abilities. Protocol requires that a worker planning to take a client's son under custody have a police warrant and accompanying officers. The CYS worker should have made formal custody arrangements before the meeting. Jane had experienced little control in the matter and appeared to feel bad about pressing charges against the young mother. Beth, the SIL director, convinced her to press charges because the young mother needed to face "appropriate repercussions" for her actions.

The officials created an unsafe emotional environment, which clearly influenced this mother's resistance. The mother had little recourse against the CYS worker's unreasonable discretion to take her child away, and her resistance appeared to stem from a place of helplessness and rage. In other words, unfair governance played a role in pushing her to act the way she did. Social ecology informs acts of resistance. In fact, Jane's ability to empathize with the mother's powerlessness appeared to fuel her misgivings about pressing charges. According to Jane, the CYS worker had cruelly abused her power. In this case, the official protocol could have safeguarded the young mother from the whim of an individual CYS worker. In contrast, as we saw in chapter 4, Nyisha and I successfully resisted an official protocol to obtain a house with the PHA. In the situation with Nyisha, following protocol would have resulted in an unjust housing denial because of a PHA error.

Depending on the situation, following an official protocol could either promote or hinder humane care for a young family. When relationships between officials and clients were compromised or oppressive, procedural protocols could not feasibly safeguard client protections. Also, disjointed hierarchy in child welfare meant that supervisors did not always hold individual workers accountable for exercising unreasonable discretion with clients. Supervisors tended to be unaware of individual worker transgressions. Procedural protocols alone were insufficient in safeguarding comprehensive care for young families.

On the ground, participants transformed official rules and policies. The protocols created an illusion of neutral governance, while participants actually socially constructed and negotiated procedures. Service provision was never a fixed or objective process.

Resisting Protocol

As detailed in the preceding chapter, Nyisha and I resisted the PHA protocol and we were successful. We avoided an official hearing, which would have taken too long—leaving Nyisha and her son homeless. In the following vignette, Jasmine and I negotiated medical services. This example provides another illustration of the challenges involved in following official procedures when these do not help clients to receive services.

On a cold day in late January, seventeen-year-old Jasmine and I trudged through the dirty, slushy snow to visit a Planned Parenthood clinic. The previous morning, I had agreed to escort her to the clinic, where she planned to get an abortion. I introduced Jasmine in chapter 2, describing an instance of her being threatened at gunpoint by an informal resident. Jasmine had a two-year-old daughter. During the car ride to the clinic, Jasmine conveyed her feelings about the abortion. While she believed she could not feasibly support another child, she also conveyed her misgivings about the procedure. Even on this cold winter day, four protesters held large signs and blocked our path to the clinic's entrance. One white middle-aged man stood closest to the entrance and asked us to take some reading materials. When we ignored him, he yelled, "Don't enter that evil place. Don't enter that place of killing!" I felt my face grow hot with anger. I was frustrated that these protesters might make more painful a situation that Jasmine already considered difficult. The only retort I managed was "Mind your own business!" After we entered, I asked Jasmine whether she was OK. She responded that she had barely noticed the protesters because she was engaged in our conversation.

After Jasmine checked in at the front desk, I asked her to select where we should sit. She chose the smaller and less crowded of the two waiting areas. Mostly African American women waited, as well as a couple of Latina and white women. I noticed two men: one white and the other black, both apparently waiting with their female partners. One Latina woman was accompanying another and translated for her. In total, the visit to the clinic lasted five hours. Jasmine appeared small as she disappeared into her puffy black coat, which she wore for the entire time we waited.

After we had waited for quite a while, an attendant at the front desk called Jasmine's name. She went up alone. As the woman flipped through Jasmine's file, it looked like something was wrong. I thought to myself, "Please let her get this procedure today." After years of accompanying youth, I was always ready for something to go wrong. Almost always, something did. I resisted the urge to jump up, and before long Jasmine walked back. She explained that Planned Parenthood did not have the paperwork from CYS, which was needed to verify half the payment for the abortion. Because of Jasmine's court-ordered status, CYS would cover half the cost for the procedure, while Jasmine's medical assistance would pay the other half.

Confusion and service mishaps almost always resulted from multiple agencies being involved in client regulation and service provision. The attendant asked Jasmine to reschedule, but instead we tried to correct the problem. Jasmine explained to me that she had watched as her caseworker set up payment with CYS over the phone. As another youth explained during an interview:

> And as much as I nag [my caseworker], it seems like [she's think-ing] "Oh, God, just leave me alone." They [caseworkers] still don't do nothing. . . . Like I'll call and harass, harass, harass. And it will still be like OK, OK, OK, just to shut me up. And you know, it's like calling and being in their face really doesn't do nothing. Because [the worker says,] "I'm going to do it later," and it slides through the door, don't feel like it, whatever.

Jasmine's observation of her worker was important because, as we have seen, clients could not often be certain whether caseworkers followed through with phone calls, paperwork, and other negotiations necessary to obtain a service.

Jasmine and I decided to call the CYS worker on my cell phone. Predictably, the call went to the worker's voice mail. I wanted to call the worker's supervisor, but Jasmine asked me to try the CYS worker once again. This time the worker answered her phone. I was pleasantly surprised. In my prior role as program manager, I had learned that CYS workers almost never directly answered their phones. Oftentimes, it would take multiple messages and several days before a call would be returned. The CYS worker seemed annoyed with my request; she emphasized that caseworkers were supposed to set up payment with her well in advance of a client's procedure. After locating Jasmine's record, the CYS worker corroborated that she had indeed already faxed the approval number to the clinic. The front desk receptionist arranged for the CYS worker to resend the information.

After several years of negotiating services, I had begun to expect misplaced paperwork, unmade phone calls, and confusion, as well as the need for repetition and persistence. Officials frequently forgot prior phone conversations and lost paperwork from earlier interactions. Finger pointing across agencies was also common, as each agent tried to avoid blame and responsibility for mishaps in the quagmire of service provision. This tactic was easy to maintain in a hybrid service environment. Multiple agencies and a cadre of officials were responsible for any particular client's care. If Jasmine and I had been unable to reach the CYS worker that day, we would have left the clinic. Jasmine would not have received the procedure.

After Jasmine saw the doctor, she learned that she was further along in her pregnancy than she had expected. Our prior persistence was even more imperative than we had originally realized. Something as minor as a lost verification number could have resulted in Jasmine's not getting an abortion and potentially even carrying her pregnancy to term. Had she left the clinic that day, she may not have returned. The arbitrariness of these multiple conditions is problematic, as is the lack of client power. For many clients, multiagency, multistep protocols resulted in service delays or a lack of services entirely. The interactions I participated in over time taught me that obtaining services required wizardry, persistence, resistance, and luck, rather than any rational or objective set of circumstances.

Next, I discuss a different form of opposition: collective resistance. Groups of youth sometimes came together to resist SIL program rules. These forms of resistance, like individual and protocol types of resistance, did not tend to result in system-level changes.

Collective Resistance

The lighting was dim. The low ceiling created a stuffy atmosphere as eight young mothers, their children, and three adult staff members crowded around a table in the basement GED classroom. This classroom was run by the SIL agency, and since it was Friday, the GED program was not in session. A SIL staff member was using the room for the afternoon "Sistahs' Event." The agency had scheduled a speaker from a sexual health program to facilitate a workshop. In the meantime, Janice, a "live-in" part-time staff member who stayed at one of the SIL apartment buildings, was going over program rules with the clients in her usual loud, direct tone. Her responsibilities included performing curfew checks and upholding the visitors policy.

Janice told the girls that if they lost or forgot their keys and were locked out, they would have to pay a fine. She did not want girls knocking on her door at 4:00 A.M. because she was a college student and needed her sleep. She continued to reiterate that curfew check was at exactly ten o'clock, also remarking that some of the girls were restricted from having visitors. These clients supposedly knew who they were. Ebony, one of the youth, asked, "Will you do me a favor? When you find a guy in my apartment, don't tell him who you are or that I'm in a program." Ebony grinned at the other girls when she made this comment, and some of them laughed. Janice responded, "Well, you know what time visiting hours are over. Just make sure he's gone, and you won't have to be embarrassed."

Another young woman asked whether they could get a larger stipend, saying that sixty-two dollars a week was not enough. "It isn't up to us," Janice replied. "CYS sets the amount." When other girls continued to complain about the stipend, Janice interrupted loudly, "These are CYS rules and we have to go by them! If we don't, y'all won't have a place to live!" One of the youth chimed in, "And you won't have a place to work." The youth erupted in laughter.

Nicole blurted out, "The program allowed me to get pregnant!" Janice ignored this comment as she continued going over various rules. There was a performance dimension to the banter, in which the youth entertained one another with humorous retorts to Janice's attempts to discipline them. Janice told the girls that clients would no longer be allowed to sit on the steps in front of their apartment building. She explained that nonprogram residents had complained to the landlord that some clients were rude and blocked the front entrance. She directed them to hang out in the park next to the building. Imani, in a voice at least as loud as Janice's, blurted out, "What can we do? You keep saying, 'Y'all can't do this. Y'all can't do that.' I always hear what I can't do, so what can I do?"

Unlike the other girls, Imani did not have a smile on her face, and there was clear frustration in her voice. While the other youth looked at each other as they retorted, Imani looked directly at Janice. An awkward pause followed. Then Janice replied, relatively subdued, "What do you want to do?" Janice explained again, "These are not our rules. These are CYS's rules." Imani answered, "You talk about respect, so why don't y'all learn to talk to us with respect?"

The politics of representation and regulation were imbued with struggle. Agents used rules as disciplining practices, and they embodied power through their modes of communication. The social positions of players mattered. Youth and their caseworkers not only revealed their social positions but constructed them through interactions. Sherene Razack (1998) maintains that we come to know ourselves and perform in ways that reproduce social hierarchies. She argues that we make social change through disrupting hegemonic ways of seeing. Hegemonic ways of seeing are commonsense perceptions about other people, views that we take as reality. Through various methods, the young women in SIL attempted to expose hypocrisy in the program's authority and in Janice's role as a mediator of program rules.

Participants enacted power through race, class, age, and gendered identities. Janice was in her early twenties, scarcely older than the young women she supervised. She was black, like most of them. She had grown up poor in the same city as her clients. In many ways Janice and the young women were in common positions at the bottom of a social hierarchy. The live-in staff members occupied the bottom of the agency's staff hierarchy because their jobs were part time and marginal. They had limited influence over program policies. In relation to both the agency and the larger society, Janice had limited power. However, she distinguished herself by asserting her authority to supervise *these* youth.

In contrast to her assertive mode of communication, Janice denied responsibility for the effects of CYS mandates. She characterized the city agency as an elusive, all-powerful entity. She suggested to the girls that they could not blame her for shortsighted CYS policies. Janice established herself as the enforcer, but not the creator, of these rules. The youth did not blindly accept Janice's attempt to depoliticize her own authority. In response to Janice's warning that if they didn't follow the rules, they would not have a place to live, one of the moms retorted that then Janice would not have a place to work. The clients pointed out Janice's vulnerability and lack of power in relation to CYS. Nicole implicated the program in her pregnancy, thereby degrading the power of the program to prevent repeat pregnancies.

The young women collectively resisted Janice; they communicated in jest and under the guise of laughter. Tensions remained just below the surface, but the mood was upbeat,. However, Imani confronted Janice directly. She appeared to be personally insulted by Janice and to perceive a collective injury to the group. Janice enforced the removal of the mothers' physical bodies from their front steps, which implied their low worth and stigmatization as youth of color. Imani was protesting the construction of her own body (and those of the other girls) as a social "problem" (Cox 2007).

Patricia Hill Collins (1998) maintains that throughout history, black women, in everyday contexts, have offered acts of resistance and critique against imposed stereotypes. In the SIL program, collective resistance occurred less frequently than individual resistance. The program created few opportunities for youth to gather together. Resistance was multidimensional, and different contexts informed these social acts. In the encounter with Janice, the girls refused to allow for one-sided surveillance. They contested both the parameters of their regulation and the authority of the enforcer. In the process, Imani fought against, while Nicole played with, the narrow and punitive representations of their bodies and characters.

Silences

For many youth, resistance was part of the everyday fabric of living in a SIL program. However, some youth deliberately disengaged and tried to fall outside the program officials' radar. These moms were underrepresented as participants in my research. The youth with whom I interacted the most were the ones who hung out in the SIL offices and wanted to participate in my research. I suspect that client disengagement was more prevalent than what I could observe directly. Because of my prior role as program manager, I knew several clients who did not participate in any program activities. Some youth told me that they deliberately avoided other SIL moms and instead made friends with outsiders. They said they stayed to themselves to avoid "drama," or infighting. I learned about this tendency from a couple of research participants and on occasion observed clients in the staff office whom I had never before encountered.

Anisa, a nineteen-year-old mom of two daughters, used silence as a strategy. I knew her well from when I was a program manager, and she was one of a few clients remaining in the program. Anisa felt pressure to meet unpredictable CYS expectations around education in order to retain her board extension. She believed that her status in the program was constantly threatened. She learned that the best way to stay out of the punitive gaze of surveillance was to remain as inconspicuous as possible.

She told me the following:

They [CYS workers] want to see you fail; they don't want to see you succeed. So they [CYS] gave me this guy [a CYS caseworker] and I barely knew him. He came to see me one time. He didn't know anything about me. The only thing he goes by is what is in my file. He doesn't know what type of mother I am to my kids. . . . I was having a problem because he was asking me what I am doing about school. And I was like, OK, right about now, I'm working. . . . And I'm waiting for my GED results. He was like, well you know, you can't work full time and stay in the program. Before him, my other CYS worker was going to let me work full time. . . . I really never had a problem with the system. I try to go by everybody's rules. I don't give anybody a hard time. Sometimes, I found myself getting scared because I don't know what's happening with my case. . . . I don't have control at all. . . . [And] we don't have an open line of communication.

Anisa's apprehension was fueled by her lack of power in affecting her status in the SIL program, as well as by an ever-changing cadre of caseworker gatekeepers. Because of her identities as head of household, mother, worker, student, and girlfriend, Anisa felt over-burdened and stressed. As a court-ordered dependent youth, Anisa negotiated services with SIL caseworkers and her CYS workers. Because of high staff turnover rates in both agencies, these work-ers changed often, and Anisa did not feel known by them. As if the floor kept moving beneath her, she was unsure about how to meet shifting expectations. Her family's stability was tenuous. Anisa lived in constant fear that her family could become homeless at any mo-ment, subject to the whim of any one of her workers. She explained:

And at one point of time, I found myself stressing, Ms. Lauren, stressing! And I thought to myself . . . I'm not doing anything wrong. . . . I'm just doing what I'm supposed to be doing. . . . But there still be times when I really be needing to talk to somebody. . . . The case manager we have now, Ms. Ebony . . . we don't have an open line of communication. It's like I can't talk to her. . . . She wouldn't understand where I'm coming from. . . . So I was like, "I see. OK, I can't talk to her. So who else am I going to talk to?" So I just might as well be quiet, stay to myself, and not talk to anybody. . . . That's what I do. I'm very quiet.

Anisa conveyed her silence and detachment as a way to cope with feeling insecure about her place in the SIL program. The lack of trust and openness she experienced with her SIL caseworker in-fluenced this coping mechanism. On the one hand, being silent was functional for Anisa because she stayed out of trouble. On the other hand, being silent took a toll on her. She wanted to open up and have workers respect her viewpoints. But she did not feel safe enough to do so. Instead, Anisa wrote poetry:

Like when I don't have no one to listen to me, I have no other choice but to write it down on paper. . . . I felt like I could not be heard at all. Like you was talking yet you was talking in silence. And when I write, I just get up, breathe in and out and I just feel so good like I got it out.

Her private expression responded to the lack of cooperative relationships with other providers and participants in the program. A common perception of threat destabilized the formation of a caring collective.

Anisa overheard Janile, her long-standing SIL live-in worker, tell another client that it was time for Anisa to leave the program. Anisa cried as she told me about this over the telephone. In an earlier interview, Anisa had professed how much she loved Janile, one person who had supported her through many personal trials. In order to avoid Janile afterward, she did not pick up her weekly stipend check, which caused financial hardship for Anisa and her family.

I recommended that she talk to Janile and express her hurt. Janile had told me on several occasions of her affection for Anisa. I believed that some sort of misunderstanding had occurred. I said, "You can't get kicked out of the program for expressing your feelings." Anisa was too scared to address Janile, so I suggested that she speak to the program manager, Jane. By the end of our conversation, she agreed. I later learned that she remained silent and did not address her hurt feelings with anyone else.

At the time of this conversation, I believed that confronting the issue would be beneficial. I was focused on helping Anisa feel empowered, and I thought that the emotional (and financial) distress could be resolved through a conversation. In retrospect, my comment—that she couldn't be kicked out for expressing feelings— was incorrect and naive. Officially, the program could not discharge a client because a staff member did not like her, but workers held grudges against particular clients, and some went to considerable lengths to cause hardship. Youth lived in an unpredictable and unsafe environment in which their status in the program was always in jeopardy.

A culture of fear and insecurity fueled Anisa's inability to communicate her feelings with SIL staff. Anisa experienced what she referred to as "posttraumatic stress disorder," as a repercussion from having been abused. She did not have a program outlet for sharing her experiences and resolving her problems. She was caught in a predicament faced by many SIL youth on board extensions. She could not voice her vulnerabilities, which might make her appear incapable of success in the program. She needed to maintain an appearance of being a good mother, a competent student, and a capable resident. Her coping response of silence was functional in the context of an unsafe and unpredictable SIL program environment. She adapted resiliently to a flawed system and SIL program, but her silence concealed her ultimate desire for nurturance and support.

Caring Collectives?

The pervasive culture of fear in the SIL program and child welfare system hindered caring relationships between staff and mothers as well as within groups of youth participants. Consistent and stable collectives were improbable in this environment. One could never be certain whom to trust. Poverty, violence, bureaucratic obstacles, resource rationing, and lack of trust all tended to foster an each-person-for-herself ideology among clients, caseworkers, and administrators. However, I witnessed short-lived moments of cooperation between mothers, as well as between mothers and staff.

In spite of the fights between clients, youth helped one another out and built each other up. Clients generally cared for one another through one-on-one interactions and, less frequently, through group collectives. The following vignette provides an example. A young mom, who had just moved into the program a week earlier, came to the program directly from the hospital after giving birth to her son. She was waiting in the Evergreen staff office for a return phone call from her SIL caseworker, as she did not yet have a phone in her apartment. She was worried about her newborn baby because there was discharge where the umbilical cord had been removed. Christy, another SIL mom, who spent a lot of time in the office, overheard my conversation with the young mom. Christy asked the other youth if she could take a look, explaining that she had two children and was "like a nurse." I offered confirmation. Christy spent a lot of time at hospitals because both of her children were medically compromised.

After observing the baby, Christy announced exuberantly that it was fine and told the mom to put a diaper over the baby's belly button. The two moms also discussed breastfeeding. The new mother was breastfeeding her baby, and Christy remarked that she had breastfed her firstborn son. Christy said this had been good for her because it made her "stomach go down," and it was also good for her son. She used to crave these onion ring chips called Scunions, but she stopped eating them because they would make her milk smell bad. The new mother appeared to be listening.

Christy changed the subject and told all of us in the room (Rebecca, the new mom, and me) about her grieving process over her father, who had died of alcoholism. She said she felt angry and would like to read a book about grief. She asked me whether I could suggest one, and I told her I would look into it. Christy's disclosure created a sense of intimacy in the room. I was surprised by her willingness to make herself vulnerable in front of this new client. Clients were usually on their guard, tending to protect their vulnerabilities, at least in group SIL settings.

I observed other instances in which mothers helped each other out. They would support each other not only emotionally or through offering advice but also with childcare assistance. Sharing babysitting obligations was common. These alliances were generally unstable, and I watched several friendships quickly deteriorate.

On one particular Halloween, several social cliques in the SIL program came together to throw a party for their children. To avoid causing financial hardship for any particular host, they decided to have the party in the office. They organized to divide the labor, as well as the purchases. A couple of youth were in charge of decorating the office with spooky spiderwebs and cardboard monsters. Others bought the candy, and still others brought homemade jerk chicken, macaroni salad, and baked beans. The youth transformed the SIL office. The children arrived in masks and costumes, along with their mothers. Everyone's spirits seemed uplifted as loud R&B and rap music, as well as savory smells, filled the air in the crowded space. One young mom brought helium-filled balloons, one for each child. At one point in the evening, a couple of youth started to argue, their voices rising. One of the girls stopped the squabble, saying that she would "squash" it because she didn't want to destroy the evening for the kids.

Moments of collectivity or kindness arose from time to time. Within the SIL program, these spaces were rare, but they point to the potential for organizationally supporting an ethos of care within the program and broader child welfare system. Next, I explore a vignette in which participants created an open and flexible forum. Directly after the rule discussion that involved Janice and several clients, a male health facilitator arrived at the basement GED room for the "Sistahs' Event." The sociocultural dynamics of the space shifted drastically once the educational session began. The shift occurred because of the facilitator's open, egalitarian style and the absence of overt surveillance from SIL workers. This transformation in power, although temporary, enabled youth to explore and create knowledge together.

Collective Knowledge and Social Critique

Scott, a relatively young, white male (apparently in his midtwenties) assumed his role as a health educator. He allowed and encouraged all participants to share their personal experiences and knowledge about sexual health. Imani's relationship to the group altered as she transformed from a resistant agent, during the previous encounter with Janice, into an active, high-spirited, and cooperative participant. The ways Scott posed questions, accepted the girls' offerings, and gently corrected misinformation encouraged participation among many of the group members. They built collective knowledge in connection to their everyday experiences and identities. The room was bustling with excitement as the youth met Scott's energetic tone.

Scott declared, "I am going to give you penises and vaginas. You are then going to match the names to the parts of the anatomy." As soon as Nicole received the worksheet, she yelled out, "Butthole." Scott responded, "Yes, you can also write down any names you know for body parts; but what is the more formal name?" Nicole replied correctly, "Anus." Throughout this opening activity, Nicole continued to blurt out words, and she sought affirmation from Scott that she was using the correct terms. Scott assisted Nicole, accepting her enthusiasm and active engagement. He announced to Janice, "This is a fun group." At the beginning of the session, a few girls, in addition to Nicole, had blurted out answers to Scott's questions.

It appeared as though they were trying to embarrass Scott and create humor. Scott reacted casually and supportively to the girls' testing. Another facilitator might have disciplined their actions as inappropriate, which would have created a very different, more closed environment.

Trust seemed to grow among the participants because the second part of the session was more serious. During a discussion about HIV/AIDS, one of the young women asked whether it was true that one could have sex with an infected person and not get the disease. Scott responded that it was rare for someone to avoid contracting HIV after repeatedly having sex with an infected partner. Erica, another young mother, said it depended on the individual's immune system. Imani countered that even with a strong immune system one could get HIV, because the virus disguised itself as the individual's cells. Scott agreed that one could contract HIV even with a strong immune system. He used the example of basketball star and businessman Earvin "Magic" Johnson, who has lived many healthy years with HIV because he has kept his immune system strong through eating well, exercising, and using medications.

Imani responded, "But he's not like us because he has all the money to buy the best medicine." Scott said that since we all live in the United States, we have access to a health-care system that provides medications for everyone. Another girl clarified that they had access to medication, but that it was the "generic type" and of lesser quality than the type Magic could afford. Other girls agreed. Imani reiterated, referring to Magic, "He is not like us. He can buy the best."

Ebony said she had heard that one in four African American women have HIV. She looked around, saying, "That is like us in this room." Scott responded that he had not seen this exact statistic. Ebony said she had seen it on a sign in the subway. Scott's voice grew more sober as he announced that he was going to be "real" with the girls. He said that AIDS was growing fastest among black women in the United States and that people used to think it was a gay disease, but "AIDS does not discriminate." Erica added that it was easier for women to get because they were dark and soft on the inside. Imani agreed, saying symptoms often didn't show up for men. Again, Scott said he was going to be "real" with them: chlamydia was an epidemic in high schools in the city. Chlamydia is spread the same way as HIV. If all of those students were to get tested for HIV, he said, it could be pretty depressing. Ebony blurted out, "I am never going to have sex again!" Imani followed up on her previous comment about symptoms not always showing up for guys, saying that one she knew developed AIDS and died. But before he passed away, he left notes to all these "young girls," telling them that he gave them AIDS. The girls had not known they were infected and had already spread it to other guys.

In this "Sistahs' Event," youth constructed knowledge jointly in relation to their identities and as a form of social critique. The youth compared the circumstances of their own lives as poor black adolescent mothers to the circumstances of Magic Johnson, a famous, wealthy black male. They highlighted the significance of gender, class, and age in shaping experiences of health and illness, as well as in mediating life and death. The local black man from Imani's neighborhood died, while Magic Johnson continued to thrive. Imani situated herself as part of the group of poor young women of color in the room. She noted the ways their collective reality differed from Magic Johnson's privileged life. Also, their access to health care was much more limited. Ebony recognized their vulnerability as a group when she related the ominous AIDS statistic.

Scott validated the youths' experiences and opened a space for them to explore their identity politics. The discussion about generic medication could be considered a metaphor for the many ways these young women understood themselves as marginalized in the United States. Sherene Razack (1998) discusses how an understanding of power as free and autonomous ignores the ways group membership alters and constrains the individual. The young women in the "Sistahs' Event" explored different health risks and access to medical care in relation to their group's constraints. Both in the preceding discussion and in the program rules discussion with Janice, Imani offered critique. She perceived Janice as disrespectful and felt that she and the other girls were stereotyped and judged. The unsafe context shaped her confrontational style with Janice. During the health lesson, she enthusiastically constructed social critique. The two discussions occurred in the same physical space on the same morning, yet the alternate social and power dynamics shaped her voice in distinct and changing ways.

Conclusion

Providers constantly evaluated clients, and the emphasis on individual rehabilitation was the norm within the SIL program. Youth were not free to communicate openly and to share their experiences, identities, and knowledge. The collective forum that occurred during the health education session was rare within the SIL program. In fact, youth more commonly resisted confinement and expressed frustration about systematic compromises to their well-being. The "Sistahs' Event" indicates that when given the space, youth reflect keenly and critically on their conditions. These youth respected each other's contributions. Also, the session provided a creative contrast to disciplinary norms within the program. This chapter has explored a range of resistances employed by youth alone, collectively, or with caseworkers (or me as an advocate). Yet even though these instances of resistance were common, opposition did not result in broad policy and governance shifts. Alliances were weak, because each individual attempted to avoid blame for structural problems in the system.

Moving from Disconnected Systems to Communities of Care

The impetus for this book began twelve years ago when I first encountered the SIL program and its participants. I began as a program
manager, and I wanted to improve the well-being of young families.
Like so many others who enter the field of child welfare service provision, I was invested in supporting children and youth to overcome
adversity and to thrive. I remain optimistic after all these years, even
after witnessing injustice and pain that I could never have foreseen.
The platform for my hopefulness has shifted. Contrary to my own
and the wider field's historical focus on the nuts and bolts of service provision, I now argue that we face a crisis of imagination and
vision. I believe in the capacity of teams of participants (including
youth, practitioners, policymakers, and researchers) to envision and
articulate more inclusive parameters for care.

When I worked as a program manager for SIL, I felt restricted in
my own ability and that of my team to imagine new ways of interacting with and caring for youth and their young children. I needed to
do my job, and I was susceptible to many pressures and limitations
that I have already described in this book. I wanted to "practice" in a
more humane way—and I couldn't figure out how my daily actions
became so disconnected from my intentions. I wasn't alone in this
dilemma. As I moved into the role of researcher-advocate, I gained
the distance and freedom to imagine new kinds of questions and to
look through different lenses. A critical feminist approach gave me
the tools to stay connected to the community I cared about while
also providing analytical options for imagining alternative ways of
looking. However, I did not envision these new directions alone;

it was through the voices of youth and caseworkers that more nuanced perspectives emerged. I was grounded in the realities of participants' daily lives, even as I gained the distance to advocate as I saw fit and to see identities and service negotiations in broader contexts. I began to consider webs of institutional relationships as my gaze shifted from one of surveillance to one that included multiple standpoints (Sprague 2005).

In ending this book, I do not complete it, because there is still much work to be done. Low-income youth of color in our U.S. urban child welfare systems face ongoing challenges that require our collective attention, care, imagination, and action (Smith 2011). As an update, I spoke briefly in December 2013 and January 2014 to a few providers and legal advocates in the city where I had studied SIL, and I reviewed current legislation concerning older youth in care. In this conclusion, I share these perspectives on SIL policies and services. Further, I suggest shifting how we diagnose the "problem" of youth care in the child welfare system. In doing so here, I also change the types of solutions that might be envisioned. I explore several recommendations that stem from my research, ideas that should be refined through conversations across communities of youth, caseworkers, providers, legal advocates, policymakers, and others. These suggestions are meant as conversation starters and as ways to spark solutions across a spectrum of creative possibilities.

Rather than focusing on individual fixes, I ask different kinds of questions. What sorts of collaborations can reduce segregation and social divisions between "privileged" youth in U.S. society and "marginalized" youth in care? What types of social connections (micro and macro) can better help youth in care gain access to multiple pathways to their versions of "good" lives? When we focus on social connectivity, we move away from viewing children as parts to be fixed and institutions as the mechanisms to fix the separate pieces. When we overfocus on one aspect of an individual client, or on one part of a system, we blind ourselves to the embedded and interconnected lives of children, youth, caseworkers, administrators, policymakers, researchers, and the rest of us in the public sphere.

Multiple Connections, Multiple Forms of Knowledge

Reforms for older youth in care require collaboration. I draw on the concept of "boundary spanning" (Kelly 1992: 254), which involves looking across disciplines, methods, and communities to inform social action and political engagement (Cosgrove and McHugh 2000). This book has modeled such an approach in the way I bridged my on-the-ground practitioner knowledge in child welfare with critical youth approaches and feminist methodology. Through bridging these forms of knowledge, I hope to offer the public more nuanced and powerful ways of understanding youth identities.

I found that a "blame game" and a culture of fear across spheres of child welfare restricted efforts to work collaboratively. When officials blamed youth for not succeeding in school or for not being responsible enough or "good enough" parents, they ignored structural problems. Their focus disregarded underfunded or fragmented child welfare policies. When administrators blamed caseworkers for ineffective service provision, they ignored the fact that caseworkers did not have the tools or the training needed to do their jobs. When judges blamed program managers for housing the SIL program in dangerous, segregated, impoverished inner-city communities, they ignored the fact that CYS did not provide enough funds to rent in "better" communities. They also ignored the fact that "better" communities commonly prevented programs for black teen moms from moving into their neighborhoods. The fragmented network of public and private regulators made it nearly impossible for a client to hold any particular provider accountable for *not* meeting responsibilities and government mandates concerning her care.

Discourses of quality control, individual responsibility, and procedural protocols maintain a facade of bureaucratic neutrality. Deeply political processes—struggles for power and inequalities in access to material and symbolic resources—remain obscured. A diminishing sector of provision fosters adversarial relations between categories of participants as each one struggles for a piece of the shrinking pie. Empowerment cannot work only on an individual level in a complex and threatening service environment; rather, we should conceive empowerment as a group mechanism (Cosgrove and McHugh

2000). Grassroots participation and social inclusion at each level of governance, including youth, caseworkers, and administrators, are needed to reform existing structures and make institutions more accountable to their communities (Wood and Roper 2004).

After completing the research for this book, I learned of a promising development in the city I had studied. Youth are empowering themselves as a group through advocacy efforts. In 2009, a local legal advocacy group initiated and supported two youth engagement collectives (which include some young moms): one for "dependent" youth in the child welfare system and the other for "delinquent" youth in the juvenile justice system. The alliances conduct research and share their experiences in order to advocate for systemic changes in child welfare and juvenile justice. The child welfare group's 2014–15 reform campaign is on SIL and independent living services for older youth in CYS. The group is surveying youth in care about their experiences and opinions regarding SIL. The group plans to use its findings to support advocacy efforts for improved SIL services.

The major limitation of my approach was that advocacy with clients did not create system-level changes. We maneuvered and developed strategies together, but within the confines and rules of the system. The anthropologist Rebecca Lester (2011: 484) poses essential questions about the role of social research: "What are the implications of our work beyond the academy? What kinds of impacts can we have—or not—in the structural systems that constrain and condition people's lives? What is our role as witnesses to inequity and suffering?" Lester encourages ethnographers to learn how to translate their work across sectors, which requires both the courage and skills to communicate with the media, politicians, community members, and policymakers. I seek partnerships with individuals in these communities who can help me translate and start their own conversations in relation to this ethnography. An ethnographic approach provides missing standpoints from youth and their service providers that are essential to informing more just policymaking and practice (Sprague 2005).

I call on policymakers to foresee what are often labeled as the "unforeseen" implications of public policies. If we pay attention to the everyday worlds of youth and their caseworkers, we can "see" how policies will work, or not, in context. I do not offer specific policy recommendations here; rather, I suggest that we change our vision of what policymakers can do. By welcoming diverse kinds of knowledge from ethnography, social mapping, visual methods, surveys, statistical analyses, and other forms into the conversation, we can make knowable the "unforeseen" implications of public policies (Small 2008; Issitt and Spence 2005). The process of policymaking should include a wider public forum for multiple standpoints, voices, and forms of knowledge.

New Diagnoses, Creative Solutions

Different theories about "the problem" of child welfare construct distinct kinds of knowledge about the nature of children and youth in the system and the role of the institution. Richard Calica, director of the Department of Children and Family Services for Illinois, offered the following analysis in an interview with University of Chicago professor of social service administration Mark Courtney:

> My aspirations for the children that we've taken into care would be the same as my own kids. . . . The problem in our field is that we don't have benchmarks. If you've got pancreatic cancer, the odds ratios are that you have a 5 percent chance of surviving the next twelve months. We don't even have a classification system in this field. . . . In terms of a diagnostic classification that would give me odds ratios of your probability of improvement success and standard treatment protocols—our field is way behind medicine. So we're in the infancy of a science. (University of Chicago, School of Social Service Administration n.d.)

I agree with Calica about wanting the same for children in care as we would want for our own children. I am sure many providers, policymakers, and child legal advocates would agree. Calica uses the analogy of individuals with pancreatic cancer for children in public care. He apparently perceives these children and youth as possessing a disease that needs to be assessed and then cured. He wants "benchmarks" for predicting which children can get better and at what rates. He compares child welfare policy and practice to medicine, but it is like a medical science that is not yet exact enough. Would Calica use the same medical and epidemiological language to describe his role as a parent to his children?

I find troubling the representations of children and youth embedded in Calica's discourse; this book has shown the damaging results (for children and institutions) of viewing children in care as illnesses to be treated. These kinds of representations remove our focus from "the problem" of structural conditions, among them urban poverty, racism, gender violence, and institutional polarization, as well as dire economic, housing, and educational situations for youth aging out of care.

I disagree with Calica's view of the institution's role. Can we use the same rules of science to organize an institution that is the mandated caregiver for abused and neglected children? The SIL youth and caseworker narratives in this book point to a need for culturally flexible program settings and caring, safe communities, which standardized benchmarks and a treatment model do not elucidate.

The disease is not in marginalized youth but rather in society: institutional patterns of oppression that limit the power of youth in care to define their own identities in the public sphere. Stigmatized representations speak in powerful ways in U.S. culture and have impact on the social policies concerning black adolescent mothers in care. Specifically, I show how programs that focus on youth "failure" and personal weaknesses restrict interventions to simply "fix these troubled girls" (Cox 2007: 55). Such agendas remove attention from fragmented institutional settings that constrain youths' abilities to define themselves and their own prerogatives. I show how young women are savvy in performing their identities, sometimes in ways that conform to sanctioned categories and sometimes in ways that resist. These performances are always situated within perceived representational contexts, because youth bodies and movements are confined by racial, gendered, sexualized, and age categories.

It is not that discourses of self-sufficiency and individual betterment have no place in a SIL program for youth and their children. Youth themselves shared ideas about wanting to be independent in ways that enabled them to provide for their children and have a "good" life. Multiple pathways should be facilitated by SIL programs, paths that connect youth to opportunities to build economic, educational, social, and professional capital. Clear communication of mutual expectations is also important. What I suggest is that a myopic focus on these individual conditions alone is detrimental because it ignores collective lives and contextual conditions that influence individual decision making. We are all embedded in social networks—interconnected—yet with differing effects. Pretending that *these* system kids should construct their futures on their own is impractical at best and stigmatizing and isolating at worst. Providers need to center both individual and collective ways of understanding youth and their needs.

Improving SIL Programs

In our conversations, young mothers described harsh living conditions before entering the SIL program. In order to survive, some youth engaged in survival tactics, involving themselves in activities such as the drug trade, prostitution, and petty theft, or they depended on older men. Some of these activities continued in the familiar zones of the SIL program, largely as a result of insufficient institutional support and the need to survive and take care of their children. Nonetheless, youth claimed repeatedly that SIL was essential to their survival, adding that without the program they would be either in prison or dead. My research suggests that if SIL resources are reduced or terminated, these young families will suffer greater insecurity and abuse. Also, because of their transitional status as youth, they will be unable to receive benefits from public systems that serve adult populations (Field 2004).

The urgency of improving SIL programs is clearly shown by the findings of Mark Courtney and Amy Dworsky (2006), who conducted the only large-scale longitudinal examination of the transition to adulthood for youth in child welfare. Their sample included 732 youth across three midwestern states. The researchers found that youth who stayed in care past age eighteen had better outcomes— they progressed further in education, had access to physical and mental health care, and had decreased risk of financial hardship and criminal justice involvement. While Courtney and Dworsky's research has helped improve policies for youth in care, Courtney and Dorota Iwaniec (2009) and Courtney, Dworsky, and Laura Napolitano (2013) suggest that we lack data on the nature of actual services provided to older youth. Without contextual knowledge, policymakers and practitioners lack guidance in how to implement innovative, higher-quality residential programs. The authors call for research on different forms of residential care, including SIL.

I offer this book as a response to this call. I share these narratives, situated in a particular historical moment, to promote conversations not only about how young families experience a SIL program but also and especially about how to improve the quality of life within SIL programs. Politically, the book occupies a tenuous space, because I both critique a SIL program and argue that SIL should be expanded and improved. SIL programs are essential to the survival of marginalized youth and their families, but the SIL program I studied is not a place where young families thrive. Research among youth in California child welfare systems found that when SIL services increased and diversified, youth found they had more options and were treated more like adults. New legislation and SIL programming were implemented in California through a collaborative team of providers, policymakers, legal advocates, and youth (Courtney, Dworsky, and Napolitano 2013).

As of this writing, in 2014, child legal advocates and SIL practitioners are fighting to keep SIL programs open in the city that I studied. Reflecting an internal shift in policy, CYS refers "dependent" children and youth to foster homes rather than to "congregate care" settings, which include SIL and group homes. One SIL provider explained to me that CYS continues to refer "delinquent" youth to SIL programs. The policy terrain for older youth in care is complex and disjointed across federal, state, and local mandates.

Federal, state, and local policies have changed for youth aging out of care since I completed my research between 2003 and 2005. My account remains pertinent because youth in the city where this study was conducted face similar, and perhaps even grimmer, circumstances than they did when I conducted the research. Unemployment rates among youth are now the highest of any subpopulation in the United States (U.S. Congress Joint Economic Committee

2010). Employment conditions are exacerbated for low-income young African America mothers in the child welfare system because their life circumstances frequently hinder or interrupt their schooling.

The broad legislative landscape for older youth in care appears to have improved since I completed my research. The federal government now grants states the *option* to provide services to youth in the child welfare system until the age of twenty-one through the Fostering Connections to Success and Increasing Adoptions Act of 2008 (Smith 2011). To persuade states to support youth in care past the age of eighteen, the federal government offers the states Title IV-E reimbursement for youth in SIL settings (this applies to both adjudicated dependent and delinquent youth). The state where my study took place adopted Fostering Connections, which offers more flexibility to youth who request services. Now a youth can remain in care if she is completing secondary education, enrolled in post-secondary or vocational education, participating in a job-readiness program, or employed at least eighty hours per month (Juvenile Law Center 2014).

According to providers in the city, CYS is ceasing client referrals to SIL because it assumes that all children and *youth* do better in family settings than in congregate care settings. Many questions remain about what care settings for youth will look like in the future. No one-size-fits-all policy can consider the capacity and needs of individual clients and whether it is in the best interests of the youth at age nineteen or twenty to move into a foster home instead of an apartment or dorm SIL setting. Reducing residential options disrespects the ability of the child welfare system to take care of "heterogeneous" groups of children and youth with unique needs, interests, and capacities (Keller, Cusick, and Courtney 2007). A legal advocate I spoke with observed that when the SIL option is taken away, the result is that nineteen- and twenty-year-old youth resist placement in foster homes and tend to leave care. From a system standpoint, CYS closes cases and saves money, which reduces the ongoing steady uptick in numbers of older youth entering care. From a youth standpoint, they likely lose a safety net and experience a difficult transition to adulthood without access to public support services.

Different child welfare silos, including federal, state, and local policies, as well as legal and provider communities, continue to work at odds with one another. Legal advocates, CYS officials, and SIL providers have different ideas about the type of programming necessary to support older youth in care, even as almost everyone wants these children and youth to do well in life. This book points to the importance of understanding "street level" policy in its many iterations because official legislation is complicated or contradicted by on-the-ground practices. Even as the specific policies have changed, the focus and approach in this book continue to be relevant today. For instance, a provider I spoke to in January 2014 noted that sometimes the youth who are most difficult to serve, who do not do well in foster homes, are placed in SIL even though relatively unstructured residences are not the best options for them. One "unforeseen" implication of the shifting nature of CYS's referral policy is unsuitable placements. The federal and state Fostering Connections legislation is not generally realized through the practices of the city's child welfare agency. Working at odds is not merely characteristic of the local nexus I studied; disjuncture inhibits collaboration and functioning across many U.S. child welfare systems (Courtney, Dworsky, and Napolitano 2013).

Mark Courtney, Amy Dworsky, and Laura Napolitano (2013: 52) suggest that "policies that in principle do justice to the needs of young adults will in practice do little without the active commitment of those charged with implementing them." The researchers emphasize the need for institutional cultures and practices to shift, so that child welfare officials can work together to better coordinate services and comprehensively support youth. Implied in their assertion is an idea that I also express in this book: researchers, policymakers, practitioners, and the public must look deeper than the legislation itself and explore participants' daily strategies that make "care." Expanding care to older youth through federal and state policies doesn't improve anyone's life if youth are being pushed out of the local system or placed in inappropriate or untenable residential situations.

An objective for the local system I studied and for child welfare more broadly is to foster "lifelong" connections between children in care and others in family-like environments. I believe SIL could be restructured through several iterations to build and sustain community while at the same time respecting the growing self-determination of youth aging out of care. SIL should be transformed from a program that segregates youth in care from other communities into a program that integrates youth across divides. Many of the caseworkers I spoke with agreed that program environments needed to be improved. Many of the youth I spoke with did not feel safe in their SIL apartments, and they desired a more caring community. Could SIL-providing agencies partner with local universities or other institutions with access to social and economic capital? Boundary spanning entails connecting across social divisions (Cosgrove and McHugh 2000). SIL apartment suites could be linked to college dormitories. Youth aging out of care, including young mothers with their children, could be placed in college communities, and different types of suites could accommodate a young family, a single youth, and youth living with roommates. Dorm communities on many college campuses already organize around common themes to coordinate purposeful living residencies. Such a hybrid SIL/collegiate community could be themed around civic engagement, child development, and child welfare justice.

Youth residents in care could simultaneously attend the college; those who are not yet ready for college could attend high school in the local community or a GED preparation program. It would be useful to have a GED option on site that could be staffed in part by college student tutors volunteering or completing work-study arrangements. Resident faculty families and caseworkers could jointly supervise the dorms and commit to collaborative educative and social justice missions.

A childcare facility could be located on site that would provide a safe educational childcare option for adolescent mothers in care, students with children, and faculty members with children. The childcare facility could support research, student internships, and coursework. Staff at the childcare site could implement collaborative opportunities for families across SIL and the college to learn about child development and parent-child interactions. Service learning courses could be facilitated at the residential site, with campaigns and projects related to child welfare and juvenile justice reform. Computer stations, community rooms, and other potential services such as a health facility could be located on site and serve the wider community.

A collaborative community model of this nature would require partnerships across diverse communities (and would involve legal contracts, adequate resources, clear stipulations for collaboration, and rules for residential living). For such an enterprise to be successful, teams of players from across legal, educational, business, government, service provider, and research communities would have to work together with youth. I believe in the potentially transformative implications of this type of intentional community. Living in a collegiate environment would help transform youth identities, as some young mothers could see themselves as college students and gain access to routes to higher education. They could become change agents in social justice campaigns. College students could also start to see themselves as social change agents or as educators through collaborating with youth in college preparatory or childcare sites.

The diverse standpoints of participants would require processes of deliberation and negotiation among the communities; the collaboration could help to break down divisions between "marginalized" and "privileged" youth and help them sustain support for one another. I do not envision this form of SIL as appropriate for all youth or young families in care, or for all college students. Multiple SIL designs should be made available based on the needs and capacities of different groups of youth in care. The theme of crossing social boundaries and partnering across communities could result in different types of innovative SIL residences. The theory underlying my proposal is that spanning boundaries of community could facilitate collaborations across populations commonly conceived of as separate. Innovative cultural processes, the sharing of social capital, and social justice campaigns could extend from these new forms of residence.

Interinstitutional Knowledge Building

Imagining new forms of boundary-spanning SIL communities is essential, particularly in the context of macro policy shifts. The

SIL program I studied was located in a specific urban context, yet we should understand the program in relation to global shifts in governance. Some authors (Beckett and Western 2001; Davis 2003; Wacquant 2002) posit a relationship between a divested welfare sector and the corresponding growth of penal structures. The U.S. prison population has grown tremendously, and the percentage of females in it is also greatly expanding. Since 1980, the number of women imprisoned in the United States has increased by 650 percent, while the rate of men's imprisonment has increased by 300 percent (Haney 2004). Increased incarceration does not correspond to increased violence; rates of crime have remained fairly consistent (Alexander 2012; Wacquant 2002). The state is distinctly and actively involved in creating this "penal welfare regime" through punitive public policies. Katherine Beckett and Bruce Western (2001) argue that reduced welfare expenditures do not indicate a shift toward reduced government intervention in social life. Rather, the change is one of more exclusionary and punitive approaches to the regulation of marginalized communities (Davis 2003; Fisher and Reese 2011).

Young people are not immune to restrictive government policies and approaches. Underresourced inner-city public schools and urban police districts increasingly use punitive policies and forms of surveillance that target low-income youth of color. These policies feed the school-to-prison pipeline—urban schools funnel marginalized youth into the justice system in growing numbers (see, e.g., Nolan 2011; and Rios 2011). When youth exit the child welfare system, they enter the criminal justice system at significantly higher rates than their peers. In fact, females who were in care have higher levels of incarceration than male peers in the general population (Smith 2011). Loïc Wacquant advises scholars to look and think across policy domains (Fisher and Reese 2011). The scholarship on global welfare and penal shifts incorporates a broader conceptual frame than does this book, but Wacquant's suggestion is pertinent here, not only in reference to global trends but also in explaining more localized changes. I conducted cross-policy analysis on a micro scale because I wanted to understand how youth and their caseworkers connected compartmentalized aspects of their lives across fragmented systems of care. We need to better understand how relationships across macrolevel and microlevel structures, policies, and institutions shape the daily lives of youth and children.

Wacquant suggests that scholarship across sectors should inform new alliances for social justice. Tracey Fisher and Ellen Reese (2011: 234) respond to Wacquant's call by specifying the contributions of feminist critical race theorists: "Building solidarity across race and gender as well as class, and challenging racialized and gender-specific stereotypes of the poor, will be critical for broadening support for welfare and for broadening opposition to the criminalization and incarceration of the poor." Increased political participation among participants across public and private sectors is imperative in fostering systems of care. Politicians must feel a push from the general populace to fund child welfare, education, housing, and childcare, as well as other efforts to eliminate poverty and inequality. Large-scale policy changes must have the backing of cross-sector social movements (see, e.g., Alexander 2012; and Fisher and Reese 2011). We need to communicate the implications of contemporary governance policies across constituents in a manner that is both convincing and urgent.

Ethnography, as a tool, allowed me to share and learn from the perspectives of youth and their caseworkers in a SIL program. I believe that their narratives can inform more humane policies and practices, and I agree with Arthur Bochner's (2001: 154) sense of the power in stories: "We must decide what calls us to stories. For some of us—I know it's true for me—finding a good way . . . to give voice to experiences that have been shrouded in silence, to bring our intellect and emotionality together . . . and to give something back to others draws us to the poetic, moral, and political side of narrative work." I hope that this book will inspire compassion, knowledge, and growth in readers as we struggle to make sense of not only the difficult worlds of these particular youth but also our relationships to these injustices. I want this account to be used by others as a tool to promote social justice and healing in ways that I cannot foresee.

Interruptions in Fieldwork

I am writing this afterword twelve years after my initial connection to young mothers and children in the Supervised Independent Living (SIL) program, and these years of investment have transformed me. I am more conscious now of the emotional and autobiographical landscape that drew me to the work. Traditionally, ethnographers reveal the fluid nature of their participants' social worlds while tending to ignore, at least in their texts, their own emotional and cognitive growth (Anderson 2006). I look back at myself as a practitioner and fieldworker and feel immense gratitude to the participants. I am thankful for their trust in sharing daily experiences with me.

I experienced what Christopher Poulos (2012) describes as "epiphany" through "interruption," which happens when some sort of engagement with the outside world causes an opening in self-perception. One of these moments occurred as I reviewed literature to prepare for this discussion and came across this articulation by Arthur Bochner (2001: 138): "I believe that the projects we undertake related to other peoples' lives are inextricably connected to the meaning and values we are working through in our own lives." I can see clearly now that I was trying to integrate my own childhood experiences that were fragmented from my adult reality. I felt an empathetic connection to children and youth whose lives were disjointed by trauma and increasingly restrictive systems. The drive to understand their strivings toward wholeness came from my own desire to integrate multiple personal and social dimensions. Early in my fieldwork, I decided to be a player in the book—my participation and advocacy offered data about how participants and I navigated the child welfare system. I was always hopeful that advocacy and research could inform better practices and policies for youth in care, but initially I was unaware of how personal this journey would be for me.

I am reminded of another "interruption" during my fieldwork. One day I visited with Janile, one of the SIL site live-ins whom I described in chapter 1 as going above and beyond her part-time job duties. Janile was older than other participants, and she both self-identified and was recognized by many clients as an influential and nurturing caretaker. I too found myself drawn to Janile's exuberant and embracing manner. I experienced refuge in the caring atmosphere she created in her apartment office at the smallest of the three SIL sites. She expressed her love for the youth and children, but she could also be demanding, as she held high expectations and required cleanliness. She expected clients to follow her rules diligently. She thought of her clients as her own children.

We began to discuss one particular client, Anisa, whom I mentioned in chapter 5 as using silence as a coping strategy. Janile told me that when we talked about Anisa, she felt as though she was talking to Anisa in person. She suggested that in my face, she could see Anisa's pain. At that moment, I had an "interruption." Until Janile showed me a metaphoric mirror, I had not realized the degree of my identification and empathy with Anisa and some of the other girls. I started to wonder why I felt more drawn to particular youth. Now I understand that I recognized aspects of the way Anisa dealt with pain. She stayed silent and tried very hard to please others and follow the rules. She had a warm and open way about her and found that many (both friends and family) had taken advantage of her kindness. I faced the world with a similar disposition, even though my life circumstances were distinct. I occupied a very different social position. Yvonne Jewkes (2011) cautions researchers to remain vigilant of the effects of power. Even when researchers identify with participants, these connections are framed through very different social contexts. Similar emotional dispositions can lead to unequal results when the researcher's life is compared to the participant's life. Our lives took place at different junctures on a social spectrum, and I had a very different set of responsibilities. I was not a low-income adolescent mother of color, struggling to support my children and myself.

Janile offered me advice in a nondirect way by sharing her own responses and emotional development. She communicated some of her personal story and the adversities she had faced when she was a young mother. These circumstances helped her to understand the struggles of her clients. Janile had faith in a higher power, which she believed helped her to remain calm on the inside at all times. She continued to say that she would do whatever she could to help her girls, but she refused to take on anyone else's pain. It took her quite some time to learn this strategy.

There were certain girls I cared about but did not understand on the same emotional level as I did other youth, such as Anisa and Nyisha. I tended to empathize most with the girls who internalized their pain. Others tended to externalize their trauma, like Olivia, mentioned in the introduction to the book, who had her son removed from her custody. I had what I perceived to be a strong relationship with Olivia, and I understood intellectually why she would react to situations with aggression. She had been raised through violence. But I did not connect emotionally to her hostile forms of coping.

I see now how my shadow, a concept Christopher Poulos (2012) extends from Carl Jung, influenced me to tell certain stories or highlight aspects of particular vignettes, without delving into other relevant issues. Poulos explains that one's shadow refers to the parts of oneself that we all possess but of which we are scared or ashamed. These parts hide in the dark, and we do not reveal them because we cannot face them. I did not always describe youth actions that I found unsavory, because I was ashamed of those parts that existed in me. Also, I was protecting the youth. Too often, officials, the media, and social scientists identified them *as* their worst behaviors. I participated in a politics of representation and did not want to add to their stigmatization.

In the book, I referred briefly to mothers who sold drugs or engaged in sex for resources, but I did not delve into these stories at length. Sometimes I heard moms scream at their children or saw them yank a little arm in a way that I found too forceful. My storytelling decisions meant that at times I did not delve fully into contradictions within individual youth and, instead, chose to focus on the incongruities in bureaucratic contexts. Carolyn Ellis (2007: 26) notes, "As researchers, we long to do ethical research that makes a difference. To come close to these goals, we constantly have to consider which questions to ask, which secrets to keep, and which truths are worth telling." My account is partial—it is linked to my autobiography and my personal take on the politics of representation. I recognize the ways I shielded the girls. Their strengths were real, but I did not convey with the same attention the behaviors that I found particularly troubling or uncourageous.

Youth and caseworkers appeared to recognize me as a caring advocate who was effective at helping the girls. I wanted to be respected as a contributor to the well-being of these young families. I felt affirmed when my old supervisor and former coworkers demanded jokingly that I come back to work with them. Both caseworkers and youth would introduce me to others using affectionate terms, as someone who was caring, helpful, and likeable. I was up front with participants about my research and the fact that I was writing a book about their experiences in the program. However, because I provided assistance and spent countless hours talking with youth, I believe that many saw me first as a mentor and advocate.

I learned how invested I was in upholding this caring and compassionate identity when I experienced a perception that was antithetical to my identity bid. I remember one poignant moment when I worked as a program manager for SIL. My supervisor and I interviewed an African American male resident of the Evergreen apartment building because he had witnessed an event reported by a client. The client accused a couple of maintenance men of sexual harassment. As we interviewed this man, he said that he had overheard some of the girls call my supervisor and me "white bitches," but he didn't agree. I felt shocked and dismayed at his comment. My supervisor and I did not react to the comment and did not talk about it afterward, and I still wonder how it affected her. I knew that my supervisor was as invested as I was in her caring professional identity. I had heard other staff members and clients affirm this identity and refer to her affectionately. Whether he had actually overheard this comment or not, I was struck by it and the memory has stayed with me for many years. I realized in that moment that the way I wanted to be perceived was not the way I would always be understood in this intense and racially unjust environment.

Was it a problem or a benefit that I commiserated so readily with some of the youth? Was it a problem or a benefit that I sought to be affirmed as a caring and effective advocate? I believe that these concerns helped me to convey a compassionate portrayal in the book and enabled my access to service contexts I would not otherwise have entered. I also believe that I was able to analyze my participation and affective process in order to make wider claims and contributions.

I am inspired by researchers who are carving out new and exciting methodological ground as they show the important roles empathy and identification play in knowledge formation, deepening our understanding of people and contexts (Bochner 2001; Jewkes 2011; Ellis 2007; Cox 2007). We exist in a world in which "objectivity" rules hegemonic over "subjectivity"—feelings are feminized and discounted by many researchers as irrational and unscientific (Bochner 2001). Jewkes (2011: 72) argues that it is faulty to assume that the researcher's emotional reflexivity necessarily undermines the validity of the research. On the contrary, "the pervasive failure of researchers to own up to empathetic feelings . . . may, at the very least, represent a missed opportunity to enrich the analysis. If we can succeed in retaining epistemological . . . rigor while at the same time 'confessing' to feelings of emotional investment do we not produce more interesting and honest knowledge?"

My emotional disposition shapes the narratives I seek out and tell, as well as my political stance. The story I tell about others in this book is integrally connected to my autobiography. Yet I also recognize the ways my account is partial.

And she sits there
As her eyes hold mine
Belly protruding
    Full
    Rounded
Young face on mamma's body
    Belly

Young lady, as her eyes shine the dreams she is waiting to exhale
To breathe freedom
What would it mean?
And she says, "The world owes me freedom."

Are you not free?
Young girl of this land of America

She says, I want only

To be
Myself.

Poverty, drugs, beaten in her face
With father's hand
Strangled

And I ask, why the anger?
Why the words, brazen from your mouth?

And your desire pours across your face

To be
Yourself.

Oh how you want
Strong words come from strong souls
Your dreams have been strangled
But hope shines in your eyes

To be
Free.

And I may ask, why pregnant at thirteen?
Abortion
Now full and pregnant at sixteen
You sold drugs to get by, raised other people's babies
Young girl
Young girl
Of infinite exposure

Your drive to get away
And to be
Oh so good
Oh be complete

To be
Myself.

—She says

To be
Myself.

—She says

To be
Free.

Oh young lady
Shining eyes on full stomach
Growing within→
A crystal sparkling
Growing within→
A baby

I wrote this poem sometime in 2001 when I worked as a program manager for the SIL program. I left it undated and untitled. An intake interview I had conducted with a pregnant youth inspired this poem. I was struck by the glow in her eyes as she talked about wanting to be free. She wanted to find a place in the world where she could become who she was meant to be. I know now that this poem flowed from a place within me that connected to this youth's yearning for escape from entrapment. I came home from work that day and wrote this poem.

Should I reveal that I too survived childhood sexual abuse?

This question surfaced repeatedly throughout the process of writing this book. I answer it here affirmatively, somewhat neatly hidden, yet also exposed in an afterword. Throughout my childhood, I experienced trauma and I often felt that I had little of value to say. I had to learn through other ways that my voice had meaning. Self-disclosure is a vulnerable act. Partially in accord with the vulnerabilities that my participants exposed to me, I too share inner workings of my own biography. Also, I share because my identity as a survivor informed my methodology and account.

As a white, able-bodied, middle-class, educated woman, I embody respectability and "normativity" in the public sphere. I move through life, interacting across institutions with my humanity intact and reflected back to me. In fact, it was my material and symbolic advantages that some of my staff (and perhaps some clients) had resented when I worked as their SIL program manager. Inside myself, I worked tirelessly to avoid a private representation, which was invisible to officials, clients, and the general public. I struggled to avoid the deviant, damaged little girl, an internal projection, who felt dirty and worthless. This projection was an aspect of my shadow (Poulos 2012). This representation had been mirrored to me by my abuser, internalized, and then incorporated through the loss of my body's integrity.

In contrast, society marked the identities and bodies of the black low-income adolescent mothers who participated in my study as deficient and as a "social problem." Aimee Cox (2007: 57) states powerfully, "Being visible as a marked body and being seen as a human being are clearly two very different things." The media, officials, and sometimes their own communities represented their identities as without respectability. How would it feel to face a social mirror that consistently denied your dignity and humanity? I connected emotionally to this struggle with respectability. It was their public dilemma and my private one. Methodologically, it is essential to investigate deeper identity connections than the outwardly apparent forms of race, class, gender, and age that ethnographers commonly explore. It was not that I experienced insider status on the dimension of social respectability but rather that I could commiserate with the struggle to make a worthy life. Jewkes (2011: 68) asserts that "knowledge, then, is not something objective and removed from our own bodies, experiences, and emotions but is created through our experiences of the world as a sensuous and affective activity."

Revealing my emotional, private self in this intellectual space is a feminist act of transgression and vulnerability. As Patricia Hill Collins explains, one can turn a condition of marginalization into a source of critical insight about how society is constructed (Chilisa and Ntseane 2010). I do this as a way to reveal how subjectivity shapes knowledge in complicated ways that transcend simplistic ascribed and chosen identity categories of race, class, gender, and age.

Because I was once a child who could not escape my abuser, I recognize what it feels like to be trapped. During fieldwork, I was disturbed by all the ways the youth remained stuck by unjust and abusive relationships and system structures outside their control. I did not reveal to participants my experience as a survivor of child sexual abuse; implicitly, this identity was part of my inquiry. My childhood experiences shaped the types of questions I asked, how I connected to participants, and also my commitment to integrity and justice for youth and children.

I feel remorse, and there are aspects of my fieldwork that I wish I had delved into more fully. I am continuing to develop as a human being, and my skills and interests as a researcher are also changing: "the wisest know that the best they can do . . . is not good enough" (quoted in Ellis 2007: 23). My account is and always will be incomplete.

I do not have any phone numbers.

I have lost touch with all youth participants.

Yes, lives were in flux, and numbers changed or were disconnected. I take ownership for my own difficulties maintaining connections. I moved away and engaged in daily life, new research, and did not keep up good correspondence. I regret this very much—I often wonder whether I would recognize one of the girls, who would now be a full-fledged adult, if I were to run into her on the street. The lives of my participants go on (at least I hope), as does mine. And I remain in the discomfort of disconnection where there was once connection. I believe that this regret stems from a sense of pain. I can never give back to these particular youth what I believe they gave to me—I learned from them courage and the importance of facing the truths of our lives together.

Notes

INTRODUCTION

1. All program and agency names are changed to protect confidentiality.

2. I want to clarify two omissions in this book: the relative absence of detailed descriptions of the children and the relative absence of mothers' comprehensive personal histories. These omissions reflect my choice to focus on service negotiation strategies. SIL mothers faced considerable oppression and abuse in family, neighborhood, and institutional settings. Yet I focus primarily on their interactions with program and bureaucratic settings, because such interactions within these contexts have been understudied. Furthermore, research has tended to individualize the accounts of trauma experienced by adolescent girls, to the detriment of a system-level understanding. I feel honored that youth welcomed me into their lives. Although I do not delve fully into the abuse and victimization that they faced outside "the system," I still want to acknowledge their courageous strivings as survivors. My omissions are in no way meant to ignore or trivialize the seriousness of injustices committed against children and youth. Rather, I am compassionately and personally committed to ending the silences that perpetuate abuse, and this book addresses one component of a complicated and much larger context of oppression.

3. Meda Chesney-Lind and Randall Shelden (2004) suggest that increasing rates of girls in the juvenile justice system do not reflect changes in crime but, rather, changes in policies, which influence more punitive school and police practices. The authors declare, "What might be called a survival or coping strategy is criminalized" (38). In other words, girls tend to run away from home to escape abusive family situations, and once on the streets they may physically assault others to protect themselves or turn to theft or prostitution in order to survive. As Sara Goodkind (2005) points out, "The rise in young women's involvement in the juvenile justice system can highlight the need to attend to how other systems are failing young women, rather than how young women are failing" (58). These researchers point to the need for changed policies and more humane interventions to support abused and neglected girls (rather than criminalize them). Prior research indicates that youth who transition to adulthood from the child welfare system are particularly at high risk of poverty, homelessness, victimization, and low educational attainment and are more likely to be underemployed or unemployed (Courtney and Heuring 2005; Courtney et al. 2001; Freundlich and Avery 2005; Reilly 2003;

Smith 2011). Studies also reveal that youth leaving care lack access to adequate physical and mental health care (Courtney et al. 2001; Reilly 2003) and that those youth who have been in care are overrepresented in the criminal justice system (Courtney and Heuring 2005; Smith 2011). Furthermore, children born to adolescent parents are more susceptible to ongoing heath challenges and poverty than those born to older parents (Mauldon 1998; Maynard 1997; Stephens, Wolf, and Batten 2003). The SIL program existed at a tenuous juncture of child welfare, juvenile justice, and other bureaucratic systems. The program served youth across the categories of *juvenile delinquent, child welfare dependent*, and *adolescent mother*.

4. Even though some audiences may not consider a twenty-year-old youth to be an adolescent, I found that caseworkers and policymakers did not differentiate between their clients by age. They referred to the entire SIL client population as *teen moms, adolescent mothers, girls*, or *young women*. I use these characterizations interchangeably throughout the book.

5. The official goal was to eventually reunify the mother with her son.

6. Across the world, black and indigenous minority groups are overrepresented in child welfare systems (Tilbury and Thoburn 2009). In the United States, African Americans are more likely to be reported for child maltreatment compared to middle-income and white Americans (Hill 2004; Tilbury and Thoburn 2009).

7. I interpreted a variety of documents for this study, including SIL program manuals, state legislation, and CYS policies. The documents revealed how official discourses defined the program and its clients. I compared these documents with data from fieldwork, which elucidated disconnection between informal and official descriptions.

8. Because many conversations took place during fieldwork and advocacy, quoted dialogue in the book is approximated from my field notes. All block quotations in the book (excluding those from published works) are transcribed from audio-recorded interviews and dialogue.

CHAPTER 1

1. The U.S. government estimates that two-fifths of eligible youth do not receive services and, generally, recipients do not have access to the full range of services provided through Chafee (Smith 2011).

2. The SIL residential director reported this figure to me. The agency raised the remaining funds required to run SIL.

3. During data collection, the number of program managers fluctuated between zero and two, depending on staffing availability. The SIL structure necessitated two program managers; one supervised the juvenile justice SIL

and the other supervised the SIL provided to adjudicated dependent moms. Even though there were two managers, clients received similar services and lived together across the three apartment buildings.

4. The program assigned SIL case managers to work from one particular site-based office, even though they moved across sites often and worked with clients who lived at other apartment buildings.

5. These staff meetings were supposed to be weekly, although they did not always occur. The objectives of the staff meetings varied and tended to include discussions of changes to program policies and practices. The meetings also provided a space for staff to voice any specific client or programmatic concerns.

6. The live-in staff position was part time. In exchange for providing after-hours oversight and conducting curfew checks, the SIL program accommodated live-in staff with an agency-leased apartment.

CHAPTER 2

1. The young man lost all SIL material resources, including the apartment he had informally shared with his girlfriend.

2. Some dependent mothers also dealt with the childcare inequality. Dependent mothers attending postsecondary schools lost their direct CYS daycare benefits. They, too, were pushed to follow ineffective protocol, applying for state-subsidized childcare assistance.

3. I am unaware of what these requirements entailed or whether they were enforced as a result of the murder.

CHAPTER 3

1. Teenagers from low-income families (who represent 38 percent of all adolescents but account for 83 percent of teenage births) are nine times more likely than teens from higher-income families to bring a pregnancy to term (Mauldon 1998). Overall, there are more white teenage mothers—44 percent—compared with 31 percent African American, 24 percent Latino, and 2 percent other racial groups. However in 1994, African Americans and Latinos had identical birthrates of 108 births per 1,000 women ages fifteen to nineteen, while white non-Latinos had a birth rate of 40 births per 1,000 (Mauldon 1998). The United States has the highest rate of births to adolescent females among postindustrial nations (Coren, Barlow, and Stewart-Brown 2003; Furstenberg 1998; Maynard 1997). Furstenberg (1998) maintains that the comparatively high rates of teenage childbearing in the United States reflect sustained levels of structural inequality.

CHAPTER 4

1. Clients transitioning from the SIL program received priority from the PHA, since they were assigned housing directly and did not have to wait. Because Nyisha was denied housing, she was not eligible for this special program.

2. At that moment, Nyisha's outlook was very positive; but I do not want to romanticize her situation. Youth like Nyisha tended to face ongoing bureaucratic and personal challenges. About a month after receiving public housing, she had to quit her job at the department store. After the PHA found out about her job, it required an increased contribution toward her rent, which she found infeasible. Furthermore, after receiving her high school diploma, Nyisha attempted to enroll at the local community college; however, her placement exams revealed that her skills were too low to qualify for even remedial courses. She would need to prepare in adult basic education classes (for which she would not receive college credits).

3. Nyisha was referring to the experience I mentioned earlier of being raped.

4. Nyisha and I had planned that she would arrive early, before the office opened, so that she could be the first client to submit her request.

CHAPTER 5

1. It is possible that her workers may have even encouraged and facilitated this act beyond just allowing her to use the fax machine.

References

Akom, Antwi A. 2008. "Black Metropolis and Mental Life: Beyond the 'Burden of "Acting White'" toward a Third Wave of Critical Racial Studies." *Anthropology and Education Quarterly* 39, no. 3: 247–65.

Alexander, Michelle. 2012. *The New Jim Crow: Mass Incarceration in the Age of Colorblindness*. New York: New Press.

Alonso, Gaston, Noel S. Anderson, Celina Su, and Jeanne Theoharis. 2009. *Our Schools Suck: Students Talk Back to a Segregated Nation on the Failures of Urban Education*. New York: New York University Press.

Anderson, Leon. 2006. "Analytic Autoethnography." *Journal of Contemporary Ethnography* 35, no. 4: 373–95.

Beckett, Katherine, and Bruce Western. 2001. "Governing Social Marginality: Welfare, Incarceration, and the Transformation of State Policy." *Punishment and Society* 3, no. 1: 43–59.

Blau, Joel, and Mimi Abramovitz. 2010. *The Dynamics of Social Welfare Policy*. New York: Oxford University Press.

Blau, Judith R., and Eric S. Brown. 2001. "Du Bois and Diasporic Identity: The Veil and the Unveiling Project." *Sociological Theory* 19, no. 2: 219–33.

Bluebond-Langner, Myra, and Jill E. Korbin. 2007. "Challenges and Opportunities in the Anthropology of Childhoods: Introduction to In Focus Section on Children, Childhoods, and Childhood Studies." *American Anthropologist* 109, no. 2: 241–46.

Bochner, Arthur P. 2001. "Narrative's Virtues." *Qualitative Inquiry* 7, no. 2: 131–57.

Carbado, Devon W. 2002. "Straight out of the Closet: Race, Gender, and Sexual Orientation." In *Crossroads, Directions, and a New Critical Theory*, edited by Francisco Valdes, Jerome McCristal Culp, and Angela P. Harris. Philadelphia: Temple University Press.

Chesney-Lind, Meda, and Randall G. Shelden. 2004. *Girls, Delinquency, and Juvenile Justice*. 3rd ed. Belmont, CA: Thomson Wadsworth.

Chilisa, Bagele, and Gabo Ntseane. 2010. "Resisting Dominant Discourses: Implications of Indigenous, African Feminist Theory and Methods for Gender and Education Research." *Gender and Education* 22, no. 6: 617–32.

CLASP (Center for Law and Social Policy). 2004. "Financing Child Welfare: What Policies Best Protect Children?" CLASP Audio Conference Series transcript, May 7. http://www.clasp.org/resources-and-publications/publication-1/0180.pdf.

Collins, Jane L., and Victoria Mayer. 2010. *Both Hands Tied: Welfare Reform and the Race to the Bottom in the Low-Wage Labor Market*. Chicago: University of Chicago Press.

Collins, Patricia Hill. 1998. *Fighting Words: Black Women and the Search for Justice*. Minneapolis: University of Minnesota Press.

————. 2000. *Black Feminist Thought: Knowledge, Consciousness, and the Politics of Empowerment*. 2nd ed. New York: Routledge.

Coren, Esther, Jane Barlow, and Sarah Stewart-Brown. 2003. "The Effectiveness of Individual and Group-Based Programmes in Improving Outcomes for Teenage Mothers and Their Children: A Systematic Review." *Journal of Adolescence* 26, no. 1: 79–103.

Cosgrove, Lisa, and Maureen McHugh. 2000. "Speaking for Ourselves: Feminist Methods and Community Psychology." *American Journal of Community Psychology* 28, no. 6: 815–38.

Courtney, Mark E., and Amy Dworsky. 2006. "Early Outcomes for Young Adults Transitioning from Out-of-Home Care in the USA." *Child and Family Social Work* 11: 209–19.

Courtney, Mark E., Amy Dworsky, and Laura Napolitano. 2013. *Providing Foster Care for Young Adults: Early Implementation of California's Fostering Connections Act*. Chicago: Chapin Hall at the University of Chicago.

Courtney, Mark E., and Darcy H. Heuring. 2005. "The Transition to Adulthood for Youth 'Aging Out' of the Foster Care System." In *On Your Own without a Net: The Transition to Adulthood for Vulnerable Populations*, edited by D. W. Osgood, E. M. Foster, C. Flanagan, and G. R. Ruth. Chicago: University of Chicago Press.

Courtney, Mark E., and Dorota Iwaniec. 2009. "Residential Care in the United States of America." In *Residential Care of Children: Comparative Perspectives*, edited by Mark E. Courtney and Dorota Iwaniec. Oxford: Oxford University Press.

Courtney, Mark E., Irving Piliavin, Andrew Grogan-Kaylor, and Ande Nesmith. 2001. "Foster Youth Transitions to Adulthood: A Longitudinal View of Youth Leaving Care." *Child Welfare* 80, no. 6: 685–718.

Cox, Aimee. 2007. "The Blacklight Project and Public Scholarship: Young Black Women Perform against and through Boundaries of Anthropology." *Transforming Anthropology* 17, no. 1: 51–64.

Crenshaw, Kim W. 1995. "Mapping the Margins: Intersectionality, Identity Politics, and Violence against Women of Color." In *Critical Race Theory: The Key Writings That Formed the Movement*, edited by K. W. Crenshaw, N. Gotanda, G. Peller, and K. Thomas. New York: New Press.

Davis, Angela. 2003. *Are Prisons Obsolete?* New York: Seven Stories.

Debold, Elizabeth, Lyn M. Brown, Susan Weseen, and Geraldine K. Brookins. 1999. "Cultivating Hardiness Zones for Adolescent Girls: A Reconceptualization of Resilience in Relationships with Caring Adults." In *Beyond Appearance: A New Look at Adolescent Girls*, edited by N. G. Johnson and M. C. Roberts. Washington, DC: American Psychological Association.

Dodson, Lisa. 2009. *The Moral Underground: How Ordinary Americans Subvert an Unfair Economy*. New York: New Press.

Dreier, Peter, John Mollenkopf, and Tom Swanstrom. 2004. *Place Matters: Metropolitics for the Twenty-First Century*. 2nd ed., rev. Lawrence: University Press of Kansas.

Du Bois, W. E. B. 1903. *The Souls of Black Folk: Essays and Sketches*. Chicago: A. C. McClurg.

Duranti, Alessandro. 1994. *From Grammar to Politics: Linguistic Anthropology in a Western Samoan Village*. Berkeley and Los Angeles: University of California Press.

Ellis, Carolyn. 2007. "Telling Secrets, Revealing Lives: Relational Ethics in Research with Intimate Others." *Qualitative Inquiry* 13, no. 1: 3–29.

Erikson, Erik H. 1999. "Youth and the Life Cycle." In *Adolescent Behavior and Society: A Book of Readings*, 5th ed., edited by R. E. Muuss, and H. D. Porton. Boston: McGraw-Hill College.

Farley, Anthony P. 2002. "The Poetics of Colorlined Space." In *Crossroads, Directions, and a New Critical Theory*, edited by Francisco Valdes, Jerome McCristal Culp, and Angela P. Harris. Philadelphia: Temple University Press.

Ferguson, James, and Akhil Gupta. 2002. "Spatializing States: Toward an Ethnography of Neoliberal Governmentality." *American Ethnologist* 29, no. 4: 981–1002.

Field, Alisa G. 2004. *Pennsylvania Judicial Deskbook: A Guide to Statutes, Judicial Decisions, and Recommended Practices for Cases Involving Dependent Children in Pennsylvania*. 4th ed. Philadelphia: Juvenile Law Center.

Fisher, Tracey, and Ellen Reese. 2011. "The Punitive Turn in Social Policies: Critical Race Feminist Reflections in the USA, Great Britain, and Beyond." *Critical Sociology* 37, no. 2: 225–36.

Freundlich, Madelyn, and Rosemary J. Avery. 2005. "Planning for Permanency for Youth in Congregate Care." *Children and Youth Services Review* 27, no. 2: 115–34.

Furstenberg, Frank. 1998. "When Will Teenage Childbearing Become a Problem? The Implications of Western Experience for Developing Countries." *Studies in Family Planning* 29, no. 2: 246–53.

Gee, James Paul. 2000. "Identity as an Analytical Lens for Research in Education." *Review of Research in Education* 25: 99–125.

Goodkind, Sara. 2005. "Gender-Specific Services in the Juvenile Justice System: A Critical Examination." *AFFILIA* 20, no. 1: 52–70.

Goodwin, Charles, and Alessandro Duranti. 1992. "Rethinking Context: An Introduction." In *Rethinking Context: Language as an Interactive Phenomenon*, edited by Alessandro Duranti and Charles Goodwin. Cambridge: Cambridge University Press.

Haney, Lynne. 1996. "Homeboys, Babies, Men in Suits: The State and the Reproduction of Male Dominance." *American Sociological Review* 61: 759–78.

———. 2004. "Gender, Welfare, and States of Punishment." Introduction to *Social Politics: International Studies in Gender, State, and Society* 11, no. 3: 333–62.

———. 2010. *Offending Women: Power, Punishment, and the Regulation of Desire*. Berkeley and Los Angeles: University of California Press.

Harris, Angela. 2000. "Race and Essentialism in Feminist Legal Theory." In *Critical Race Theory: The Cutting Edge*, edited by Richard Delgado and Jean Stefancic. Philadelphia: Temple University Press.

Herzfeld, Michael. 2005. "Political Optics and the Occlusion of Intimate Knowledge." *American Anthropologist* 107, no. 3: 369–76.

Hill, Robert B. 2004. "Institutional Racism in Child Welfare." *Race and Society* 7, no. 1: 17–33.

Issitt, Mary, and Jean Spence. 2005. "Practitioner Knowledge and the Problem of Evidence Based Research Policy and Practice." *Youth and Policy* 88: 63–82.

Iversen, Roberta R. 2004. "Voices from the Middle: How Performance Funding Impacts Workforce Organizations, Professionals, and Customers." *Journal of Sociology and Social Welfare* 31, no. 2: 125–56.

Jewkes, Yvonne. 2011. "Autoethnography an Emotion as Intellectual Resources: Doing Prison Research Differently." *Qualitative Inquiry* 18, no. 1: 63–75.

Jones, Nikki. 2010. *Between Good and Ghetto: African American Girls and Inner-City Violence*. New Brunswick, NJ: Rutgers University Press.

Juvenile Law Center. 2012. "Reproductive Rights, Pregnancy, and Parenting: Welfare Benefits for Teen Parents." http://www.jlc.org/resources/fact-sheets/welfare-benefits-teen-parents.

———. 2014. "Fostering Connections to Success Act's Older Youth Extensions in Pennsylvania." http://www.jlc.org/fosteringconnections.

Kantor, Harvey, and Barbara Brenzel. 1992. "Urban Education and the 'Truly Disadvantaged': The Historical Roots of the Contemporary Crisis, 1945–1990." *Teachers College Record* 94, no. 2: 278–314.

Katz, Michael B. 1989. *The Undeserving Poor: From the War on Poverty to the War on Welfare.* New York: Pantheon.

———. 2001. *The Price of Citizenship: Redefining the American Welfare State.* New York: Metropolitan.

Keller, Thomas E., Gretchen R. Cusick, and Mark E. Courtney. 2007. "Approaching the Transition to Adulthood: Distinctive Profiles of Adolescents Aging Out of the Child Welfare System." *Social Service Review* 81, no. 3: 453–84.

Kelly, James G. 1992. "On Teaching the Practice of Prevention: Integrating the Concept of Interdependence." In *The Present and Future of Prevention: In Honor of George W. Albee,* edited by Marc Keller, Stephen E. Goldston, and Justin M. Joffe. London: Sage.

Kingfisher, Catherine. 2002. "Neoliberalism I: Discourses of Personhood and Welfare Reform." In *Western Welfare in Decline: Globalization and Women's Poverty,* edited by Catherine Kingfisher. Philadelphia: University of Pennsylvania Press.

Korbin, Jill, and Eileen Anderson-Fye. 2011. "Adolescence Matters: Practice and Policy-Relevant Research and Engagement in Psychological Anthropology." *Ethos* 39, no. 4: 415–25.

Kunzel, Regina. 1993. *Fallen Women, Problem Girls: Unmarried Mothers and the Professionalization of Social Work, 1890–1945.* New Haven, CT: Yale University Press.

Lesko, Nancy. 1990. "Curriculum Differentiation as Social Redemption: The Case of School-Aged Mothers." In *Curriculum Differentiation/Interpretive Studies in U.S. Secondary Schools,* edited by R. Page and L. Valli. Albany: State University of New York Press.

———. 1995. "The 'Leaky Needs' of School-Aged Mothers: An Examination of U.S. Programs and Policies." *Curriculum Inquiry* 25, no. 2: 177–205.

Lester, Rebecca. 2011. "How Do I Code for Black Fingernail Polish? Finding the Missing Adolescent in Managed Mental Health Care Practice." *Ethos* 39, no. 4: 481–96.

Lipsky, Michael. 1980. *Dilemmas of the Individual in Public Services.* New York: Russell Sage Foundation.

Littlechild, Brian. 2008. "Child Protection Social Work: Risks of Fears and Fears of Risks—Impossible Tasks from Impossible Goals." *Social Policy and Administration* 42, no. 6: 662–75.

Luthar, Suniya, and Dante Cicchetti. 2000. "The Construct of Resilience: Implications for Interventions and Social Policies." *Development and Psychopathology* 12, no. 4: 857–85.

Luttrell, Wendy. 2003. *Pregnant Bodies, Fertile Minds: Gender, Race, and the Schooling of Pregnant Teens.* New York: Routledge.

MacKinnon, Catherine A. 2002. "Keeping It Real: On Anti-'essentialism.'" In *Crossroads, Directions, and a New Critical Theory*, edited by Francisco Valdes, Jerome McCristal Culp, and Angela P. Harris. Philadelphia: Temple University Press.

Mattingly, Cheryl. 2008. "Reading Minds and Telling Tales in a Cultural Borderland." *Ethos* 36, no. 1: 136–54.

Mauldon, Jane. 1998. "Families Started by Teenagers." In *All Our Families: New Policies for a New Century*, edited by Mary Ann Mason, Arlene Skolnick, and Stephen D. Sugarman. New York: Oxford University Press.

Maynard, Rebecca A. 1997. *Kids Having Kids: Economic Costs and Social Consequences of Teen Pregnancy*. Washington, DC: Urban Institute Press.

Miller, Patricia H. 2006. "Contemporary Perspectives from Human Development: Implications for Feminist Scholarship." *Signs: Journal of Women in Culture and Society* 31, no. 2: 445–69.

Mohl, Raymond A. 1993. "Shifting Patterns of American Urban Policy since 1900." In *Urban Policy in Twentieth-Century America*, edited by Arnold R. Hirsch and Raymond A. Mohl. New Brunswick, NJ: Rutgers University Press.

Morgen, Sandra, Joan Acker, and Jill Weigt. 2010. *Stretched Thin: Poor Families, Welfare Work, and Welfare Reform*. Ithaca, NY: Cornell University Press.

Nakkula, Michael J., and Eric Toshalis. 2008. *Understanding Youth: Adolescent Development for Educators*. Cambridge, MA: Harvard Education Press.

Nolan, Kathleen. 2011. *Police in the Hallways: Discipline in an Urban High School*. Minneapolis: University of Minnesota Press.

Olsson, Craig A., Lyndal Bond, Jane M. Burns, Dianne A. Vella-Brodrick, and Susan M. Sawyer. 2003. "Adolescent Resilience: A Concept Analysis." *Journal of Adolescence* 26: 1–11.

Pearce, Diana M. 1993. "'Children Having Children': Teenage Pregnancy and Public Policy from the Women's Perspective." In *The Politics of Pregnancy: Adolescent Sexuality and Public Policy*, edited by Annette Lawson and Deborah L. Rhode. New Haven, CT: Yale University Press.

Phoenix, Ann. 1993. "The Social Construction of Teenage Motherhood: A Black and White Issue?" In *The Politics of Pregnancy: Adolescent Sexuality and Public Policy*, edited by Annette Lawson and Deborah L. Rhode. New Haven, CT: Yale University Press.

Pillow, Wanda S. 2004. *Unfit Subjects: Educational Policy and the Teen Mother*. New York: RoutledgeFalmer.

Pillow, Wanda S., and Cris Mayo. 2012. "Feminist Ethnography: Histories, Challenges, and Possibilities." In *Handbook of Feminist Research: Theory and Praxis*, 2nd ed., edited by S. N. Hesse-Biber. London: Sage.

Poulos, Christopher N. 2012. "Life, Interrupted." *Qualitative Inquiry* 18, no. 4: 323–32.

Prussing, Erica. 2008. "Sobriety and Its Cultural Politics: An Ethnographer's Perspective on 'Culturally Appropriate' Addiction Services in Native North America." *Ethos* 36, no. 3: 354–75.

Razack, Sherene H. 1998. *Looking White People in the Eye: Gender, Race, and Culture in Courtrooms and Classrooms*. Toronto: University of Toronto Press.

Reilly, Thom. 2003. "Transition from Care: Status and Outcomes of Youth Who Age Out of Foster Care." *Child Welfare League of America* 82, no. 6: 727–46.

Rhode, Deborah L., and Annette Lawson. 1993. Introduction to *The Politics of Pregnancy: Adolescent Sexuality and Public Policy*, edited by Annette Lawson and Deborah L. Rhode. New Haven, CT: Yale University Press.

Ridzi, Frank. 2009. *Selling Welfare Reform: Work-First and the New Common Sense of Employment*. New York: New York University Press.

Rios, Victor. 2011. *Punished: Policing the Lives of Black and Latino Boys*. New York: New York University Press.

Rose, Nikolas. 1999. *Powers of Freedom: Reframing Political Thought*. Cambridge: Cambridge University Press.

Rutman, Deborah, Susan Strega, Marilyn Callahan, and Lena Dominelli. 2002. "'Undeserving' Mothers? Practitioners' Experiences Working with Young Mothers in/from Care." *Child and Family Social Work* 7, no. 3: 149–59.

Rutter, Michael. 1993. "Resilience: Some Conceptual Considerations." *Journal of Adolescent Health* 14: 626–31.

Rylko-Bauer, Barbara, Merrill Singer, and John Van Willigen. 2006. "Reclaiming Applied Anthropology: Its Past, Present, and Future." *American Anthropologist* 108, no. 1: 178–90.

Sanjek, Roger. 2004. "Going Public: Responsibilities and Strategies in the Aftermath of Ethnography." *Human Organization* 63, no. 4: 444–56.

Scott, James C. 1990. *Domination and the Arts of Resistance: Hidden Transcripts*. New Haven, CT: Yale University Press.

———. 1998. *Seeing Like a State: How Certain Schemes to Improve the Human Condition Have Failed*. New Haven, CT: Yale University Press.

Small, Mario L. 2008. "Lost in Translation: How Not to Make Qualitative Research More Scientific." In *Workshop on Interdisciplinary Standards for Systematic Qualitative Research*, edited by Michèle Lamont and Patricia White. Washington, DC: National Science Foundation.

Smith, Dorothy. 2008. "From the 14th Floor to the Sidewalk: Writing Sociology at Ground Level." *Sociological Inquiry* 78, no. 3: 417–22.

Smith, Wendy B. 2011. *Youth Leaving Foster Care: A Developmental, Relationship-Based Approach to Practice.* Oxford: Oxford University Press.

Solinger, Rickie. 1992. *Wake Up Little Susie: Single Pregnancy and Race before Roe v. Wade.* New York: Routledge.

Spencer, Margaret Beale. 2006. "Phenomenology and Ecological Systems Theory: Development of Diverse Groups." In *Handbook of Child Psychology.* Vol. 1, *Theoretical Models of Human Development,* 6th ed., edited by W. Damon and R. Lerner. New York: Wiley.

Spencer, Margaret Beale, V. Harpalani, E. Cassidy, C. Y. Jacobs, S. Donde, T. N. Goss, M. Munoz Miller, N. Charles, and S. Wilson. 2006. "Understanding Vulnerability and Resilience from a Normative Developmental Perspective: Implications for Racially and Ethnically Diverse Youth." In *Developmental Psychopathology: Theory and Method.* Vol. 1, 2nd ed., edited by D. Cicchetti and D. J. Cohen. Hoboken, NJ: Wiley.

Spencer, Margaret Beale, V. Harpalani, S. Fegley, T. Dell'Angelo, and G. Seaton. 2003. "Identity, Self, and Peers in Context: A Culturally-Sensitive, Developmental Framework for Analysis." In *Handbook of Applied Developmental Science: Promoting Positive Child, Adolescent, and Family Development through Research, Policies, and Programs.* Vol. 1, edited by R. M. Lerner, F. Jacobs, and D. Wertlieb. Thousand Oaks, CA: Sage.

Spencer, Margaret Beale, L. J. Silver, G. Seaton, S. R. Tucker, M. Cunningham, and V. Harpalani. 2001. "Race and Gender Influences on Teen Parenting: An Identity-Focused Cultural-Ecological Perspective." In *Adolescence and Education,* edited by T. Urdan and F. Pajares. Greenwich, CT: Information Age.

Sprague, Joey. 2005. *Feminist Methodologies for Critical Researchers: Bridging Differences.* New York: Altamira.

Stephens, S. A., Wendy C. Wolf, and Susan T. Batten. 2003. "Strengthening School-Based Programs for Teen Parents: Challenges and Solutions." *Prevention Researcher* 10, no. 3: 5–8.

Stephens, Sharon. 1995. "Children and the Politics of Culture in 'Late Capitalism.'" Introduction to *Children and the Politics of Culture,* edited by Sharon Stevens. Princeton, NJ: Princeton University Press.

Strauss, Claudia, and Naomi Quinn. 1997. *A Cognitive Theory of Cultural Meaning.* New York: Cambridge University Press.

Sugrue, Tom J. 1999. "Poor Families in an Era of Urban Transformation: The 'Underclass' Family in Myth and Reality." In *American Families: A Multicultural Reader,* edited by S. Coontz. New York: Routledge.

Tilbury, Clare, and June Thoburn. 2009. "Using Racial Disproportionality and Disparity Indicators to Measure Child Welfare Outcomes." *Children and Youth Services Review* 31, no. 10: 1101–6.

Tilton, Jennifer. 2010. *Dangerous or Endangered? Race and the Politics of Youth in Urban America*. New York: New York University Press.

Ungar, Michael. 2007. "Grow 'Em Strong: Conceptual Challenges in Researching Childhood Resilience." In *Representing Youth: Methodological Issues in Critical Youth Studies*, edited by A. L. Best. New York: New York University Press.

University of Chicago, School of Social Service Administration. n.d. "Extended Conversation: Child Welfare and Its Limits." http://ssa.uchicago.edu/extended-conversation-child-welfare-and-its-limits.

U.S. Congress Joint Economic Committee. 2010. "Understanding the Economy: Unemployment among Young Workers." http://www.jec.senate.gov/public/index.cfm?a=Files. Serve&File_id=adaef8ob-d1f3-479c-97e7-727f4c0d9ce6.

Valdes, Francisco, Jerome McCristal Culp, and Angela P. Harris. 2002. "Battles Waged, Won, and Lost: Critical Race Theory in Hard Times." Introduction to *Crossroads, Directions, and a New Critical Theory*, edited by Francisco Valdes, Jerome McCristal Culp, and Angela P. Harris. Philadelphia: Temple University Press.

Wacquant, Loïc. 2002. "The Curious Eclipse of Prison Ethnography in the Age of Mass Incarceration." *Ethnography* 3, no. 4: 371–97.

Walkerdine, Valerie. 2006. "Workers in the New Economy: Transformation as Border Crossing." *Ethos* 34, no. 1: 10–41.

Wood, Geoffrey, and Ian Roper. 2004. "Towards a Revitalisation of the Public." In *Contesting Public Sector Reforms: Critical Perspectives, International Debates*, edited by Pauline Dibben, Geoffrey Wood, and Ian Roper. New York: Palgrave Macmillan.

Index

Criminality, youth associated with, 89
Critical standpoints, 15–17
Critical youth ethnography, 16–17, 155
Cultural scripts, 118–19; conflicting, 124
Culture-of-poverty model, 70–71

Dangerous living environment, 58–59, 120–21; breakdown of familiar zone in, 73–75, 76; coping with, 50–53, 55–58; failure to focus on, 87–88; lack of protection in, 67–69; resiliency in, 70–73
Dangerous or Endangered? (Tilton), 89
Delinquency, 89–90; manipulation into, 106, 107
Delinquent youth, 5, 88–91; publicly regulated versus community-based group homes for, 11
DeLuca, Stefanie, 70–71
Dependency, 89–90; meeting definition of, 96–97; perpetuating, 40
Dependent youth, 88–91; SIL and child welfare services for, 5
Deserving poor model, 91–92; for job-training program, 100
Disconnected youth, 3
Disengagement, 143–47
Documentation, 7; requirements for, 37–38
Dodson, Lisa, 52–53, 53
Domestic violence, 24, 55–56, 83, 86–87
Dominant, 79
Double consciousness concept, 127–28
Dreier, Peter, 2, 49, 70–71

Drug dealers, 50, 136
Drugs: client discharge over, 41–42; eviction for, 80; in victimization of children, 89
Du Bois, W. E. B., double consciousness concept of, 127–28
Dworsky, Amy, 6, 159–60, 162

Education: collaborative community for, 162–64; health, 149–52
Education programs: GED, 18, 31–32, 59, 63, 85–86; negotiating compliance with, 62–64; required participation in, 59; as requirement for extended child welfare services, 91–93
Ellis, Carolyn, 169, 171
Empowerment, as group mechanism, 155–56
Empowerment narrative, 124, 128
Endangerment narratives, 89–90
Entrapment, 4
Environment, importance of, 69–73
Escalation, 135–37
Ethnography, 3; feminist, 15–16, 153–54, 174–75; institutional, 13; role of, 156; as tool, 166
Exclusionary policies, 165

Failure: claiming responsibility for, 84–85; focus on, 158; girls as, 48; learning from, 43; as social construct, 62, 88
Familiar zones, 17–18, 53–55, 76; breakdown of, 73–75, 76; coping in, 59–62; implications of, 55–59; in impression management, 62–63; rebellion in, 19; regulatory techniques and, 64–67
Farley, Anthony P., 87, 110, 125–26
Fear, culture of, 66–67, 126;

Personal Responsibility and Work Opportunity Reconciliation Act of 1996, 97
Pillow, Wanda, 13, 15, 88–89
Poulos, Christopher, 167, 169, 174
Power dynamics, 87, 151–52
Probationary status, 106
Probation officer (PO), 10, 24, 42; negotiating schooling requirement with, 62–64
Problem solving, comprehensive, 42–44
Procedural protocols. *See* Protocols
Program environment discrepancies, 21–22
Program inequalities, 17, 45
Program managers: diversified role of, 26; responsibilities of, 24–25; social distance from caseworkers of, 30–34
Program rules: collective resistance to, 140–43
Protocols: cumbersome, 117–18, 119; for removing client's child, 136–37; resisting, 138–40; rigid, 128
Public housing, 108; dead end, 73; qualification for, 108
Public Housing Authority (PHA), 19; negotiating with, 108–29
Public policies, unforeseen implications of, 156–57
Public services outsourcing, 7–8
Punitive approaches, 165

Race constructs, 15–17
Race identities, 126–28; good and bad, 110–11
Razack, Sherene H., 15, 141, 151
Reese, Ellen, 6, 165, 166
Regulation, politics of, 140–42
Regulators, multiple, 41–42

Regulatory techniques, familiar zones and, 64–67
Representations: contradictory, 76–77; distorted, 2–3; politics of, 140–42
Researcher-advocate standpoint, 12–15
Researchers: emotional dispositions of, 168–75; reflexivity of, 15
Residential director, responsibilities of, 25
Resiliency, 61, 106–7; changing, 62; cultural, 5; environment and, 69–73; traditional theories of, 61–62
Resistance, 10–11, 19; by addressing higher-ups, 133–35; collective, 140–43; definition of, 130; escalation of, 135–37; individual, 130–33; against protocol, 138–40
Respect, 116, 142, 145, 170
Respectability, 174
Responsibility: of caseworkers and administrators, 37–41; of client, 77–103; for getting needs met, 124; individual, 102–3; for own behavior, 79–85
Responsibility narratives, 83, 95–98
Responsible workers, producing, 98–101
Reynolds, Lisa, 70–71
Ridzi, Frank, 83, 87
Rios, Victor, 13, 15, 16–17, 165
Risk management, comprehensive, 43–44
Rose, Nikolas, 104, 125
Rosenbaum, James E., 70–71
Rule-breaking behaviors: with informal residents, 49–53; punishment for, 67
Rules, as disciplining practices, 141